Peace Of Mind
Is
A Piece Of Cake

our perception of an event will not be the same as someone else's

by

Michael Mallows
&
Joseph Sinclair

Illustrated by **Yaron Livay**

Crown House Publishing Limited

First published in the UK by

Crown House Publishing
Crown Buildings
Bancyfelin
Carmarthen
Wales

First published 1998.

British Library of Cataloguing-in-Publication Data
A catalogue entry for this book is available
from the British Library.

ISBN 1899836241

Printed and bound in Wales by
WBC Book Manufacturers,
Waterton Industrial Estate,
Bridgend, Mid Glamorgan.

Biographies

Michael Mallows is a management trainer, a consultant, and a psychotherapist. In 1980 he founded the Social Effectiveness Training Agency (SET) which works with groups, teams, managers and organisations all over the world. He comes from a background of Co-counselling, Transactional Analysis (TA) and Neuro-Linguistic Programming (NLP) and has more recently integrated the Enneagram into much of his training. A previously published work, *The Power to Use NLP*, was based on his Power^2 personal development programme which teaches that we^2 can empower each other in our relationships.

Joseph Sinclair's successful shipping industry background provided the basis for his earlier writings, with published books on refrigerated transport and the history of military transport. His revised and updated book on refrigerated transport is being republished this year. He has been a member of the Institute for Transactional Analysis, the International Co-counselling Community, and the Institute for Neuro-Linguistic Programming, and is the author of *An ABC of NLP*. He is a member of the Association for Humanistic Psychology.

Yaron Livay is a man with a double identity. At home in Israel he is one of the country's most successful chartered accountants. In semi-retirement in England he is a successful artist and print maker whose work has been bought by, among others, the Victoria and Albert and the Imperial War museums. His hand-printed, limited-edition books are highly prized (and highly priced). His venture into the art world began in the 1950s when, following military service in Israel's navy, he began to draw cartoons for the Israeli press. His most recent work is *The World Upside Down Alphabet* which perfectly reflects his jokey and cynical humour.

Contents

List Of Figures

Introduction

He who has health has hope;
and he who has hope has everything.
[Arab proverb]

This is the first in a new series of personal development books. Without pretending that there are any easy answers, and without getting too complex, this series offers suggestions for challenging and changing yourself, and relating to and communicating with others in responsible, respectful and effective ways.

We explore environmental and behavioural factors along with skills and capabilities for effecting positive change. We ask you to think about the beliefs and values that keep you trapped or can help release you from habits and patterns that no longer serve you.

When reading this book, think about the kind of person you want to become, and the relationships you want to have with yourself in the dead of night, and with other people in the cold light of day.

Chapter One

What Is Stress?

*Stress is the price your body pays when
life is not the way you'd like it to be*

> ## *Stress is the price your body pays when*
> ## *life is not the way you'd like it to be*

And it's a high price indeed.

Mention the word stress in conversation and the chances are that whoever you are speaking to will imagine something harmful or unpleasant. Stress is generally regarded as a health hazard and an obstacle to happiness, and the vast number of books on the subject have, by and large, done nothing to dispel this illusion. Indeed, people nowadays generally attribute many of their physical and mental problems to stress.

Yet there is no reason why stress should be regarded so negatively. Stress, in itself, is a natural response to real or potential threats in our environment. We have survived and evolved because we developed the "fight or flight" response. In the primeval rainforest the bottom-line question in response to a disturbance in the undergrowth was quite simple: "Is that lunch, or am I?"

Survival depended on answering the question, then moving in or moving on, depending upon how hungry or how afraid we felt.

At the end of the twentieth century we are seldom faced with sabre-toothed tigers and, road rage, terrorists, muggers and sundry other pressures notwithstanding, few of our conflicts, in the western world at least, are life and death choices. We need to deal with the pressures of today, from the traffic jam to the bullying boss, from troubled teens to ailing elders, as effectively as we can. Regrettably, many people think that anger, vociferousness, aggressiveness and attack will make them effective. In the short term they may be right, in the long term they may be making life-threatening choices.

Stress, in itself, is natural and not necessarily detrimental to our health. On occasion, the absence of stress might be more harmful than the stress itself, as when facing the prehistoric sabre-toothed tiger or its present-day equivalent. Stress, after all, is not "something out there": it is within ourselves, albeit conjured up by our perception of "something out there". And, since it is inside us, we have the ability to deal with it within ourselves, if only by the simple expedient of changing our perception of it. *We can choose to regard stress positively rather than negatively.*

Flight is the most frequent method of escaping perceived stress: flight into fantasy (TV, particularly soap operas); flight into addictions (drugs and alcohol); flight from one's environment (leaving a job or moving home). It is rarer to find the "sufferers" seeking relief by changing their perception of the stress. Yet this is not only the more effective way of achieving the desired end, it produces additional and unexpected benefits. It enables one to use the stress in a positive and constructive manner.

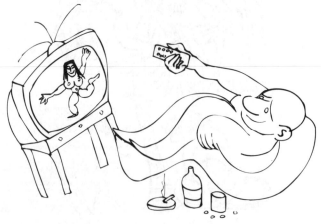

Without stress, the athlete could lose his/her competitive edge; the student would probably achieve lower examination grades; the sales representative might get fewer orders. Without stress we might even be reluctant to leave our beds in the morning: we would be bored and lethargic. It is *excessive* stress, *negative stress*, which needs to be faced and defeated.

> ### *Negative stress is interest paid*
> ### *on trouble before it becomes due*

One of the foremost writers on stress, Dr Hans Selye, developed a very useful vocabulary on the subject. In his classic work [*The Stress of Life*, 1956], he distinguishes between *eustress* (which is pleasant and desirable) and *distress* (which is harmful and unpleasant). Stress, according to Selye, *"is the nonspecific response of the body to any demand, whether it is caused by, or results in, pleasant or unpleasant conditions."*

A stress reaction as the nonspecific response of the body to any demand made upon it can have good or bad causes, and create good or bad effects. Stress should not and cannot be avoided: non-excessive stress is, like body temperature, a natural occurrence in the body.

Irritability, hyperexcitation, depression, a pounding heart, dryness of throat or mouth, impulsive behaviour or emotional instability, the urge to run, hide, cry, an inability to concentrate, feelings of unreality, weakness, dizziness, loss of energy, nonspecific anxiety, insomnia, trembling or nervous tics, high-pitched nervous laughter, stuttering, grinding the teeth, sweating, migraine headaches – all the above are signs of stress! According to Selye, these danger signals can be measured by adrenalin levels in the blood.

And while stress, of itself, does not cause health problems, unresolved stress, recurrent stressors, or "triggers" (those things or events which cause us to experience stress), will aggravate an existing health condition. Negative stress will intensify a headache in a migraine sufferer, it can provoke an attack of asthma in an asthmatic, or a stroke in someone suffering from high blood pressure.

Concern about stress leads to anxiety. Anxiety is a state of health; stress is not. We make the mistake of confusing the stress with the anxiety. Financial concerns, urban frustrations, boredom, ageing, ill health, bereavement, occupational demands, are often perceived as stress when in fact they are causes of stress.

In fact, we all have different stressors even though we may react to them in similar ways; or we have similar stressors and react to them differently.

It is the connotations that we place on our stressors, the meanings they have for us, which will control the ways in which we react to them. Our perception of an event will not necessarily be the same as someone else's; nor will our perceptions of the implications of that event. What causes us to feel bad, or unhappy, or guilty, might not stress another person at all: might, indeed, fill them with joy.

our perception of an event will not be the same as someone else's

Often people who feel trapped by their situation are prisoners of their own limiting belief systems. Trapped in the doldrums of fixed beliefs, a sargasso mind drags them into depths of despair: thoughts spin out of control, creating eddies of victim consciousness. We make demands on our bodies, and our bodies will, inevitably, demand recompense, which narrows the perspective even further. This book offers keys for unlocking the mind and unravelling some of the tangled and intertwined beliefs that reinforce the feelings of powerlessness which underpin most stress.

Although we suggest a number of simple techniques for dealing with stress before, during and after it happens, we offer no easy answers.

What we mean by this is that you must take responsibility for attaining, regaining or maintaining your own well-being. All too often we experience life coming at us head on. We see everyone else as at fault. They cause our pain (or pleasure), and we simply enjoy or endure the effects. Worse, we *become* the effects and our body demands we do something about it before it's too late.

Sometimes people don't realise just how ruinous those effects are until the body or mind eventually conveys the message "Enough is enough!" and gives up on us. Stress is not just stressful, it can be lethal! If you are going to "Get it Right", you must accept *your* contribution to your ongoing, problematic stress state.

Stressbuster
Breathe in slowly and deeply.
Imagine the "in" breaths as energy entering,
and the "out" breaths as stress leaving your body.

Questionnaire

Try answering these questions to establish your stress responses. There are no marks, no rewards, no right or wrong answers, but if you find yourself answering "yes" to any of the first sixteen questions, or "no" to the last two, we are sure you will find this book helpful.

1. Do you ever feel "unable to cope"?
2. Do you get irritated when someone is (a) slow to respond to you (b) keeps you hanging on the 'phone (c) walks too slowly for you?
3. Do you help people out when you'd rather not?
4. Do you chastise yourself for falling short of your own high standards?
5. Would you prefer not to ask for help?
6. When driving a car, do you get annoyed when (a) a driver in front of you goes too slowly (b) a driver behind you "tailgates" you (c) drivers overtake you?
7. Do you ever worry about not being able to sleep?
8. Are you unable to relax when there's nothing specific to do? Do you feel guilty or bored at doing nothing?
9. Do faults and blemishes irritate you?
10. Do you react strongly to being interrupted?
11. Do you fret about problems because you can't let go?
12. Do you try to avoid conflict?
13. Are you unable to leave your work behind you at "closing time"? Do you take it home with you?
14. Do you have any drug or tobacco addictions?
15. Do you "queue-hop" at the check-out counters of your super-market, or the check-in counters at the airport?
16. Do you count your queue neighbour's basket items at the "maximum items" check-out counter?
17. Do you take regular exercise?
18. Do you relax with any spare time activities or hobbies?

Chapter Two

Stress In Your Life

Stress is a survival strategy that
may be outdated and overrated

**Stress is a survival strategy that
may be outdated and overrated**

All change is potentially stressful. Twenty-four centuries ago
Hippocrates wrote:

*"It is changes that are chiefly responsible for diseases,
especially the greatest changes, the violent
alterations both in the seasons and in other things."*

There are three main divisions of stressors, those factors which
trigger the internal sequence that we experience as tension or
anxiety. First there are the general stressors which affect everyone,
such as war, strikes, famines and floods, over which the individual may have little or no influence. Secondly there are societal
stressors involving, for example, industry, the workplace, a social
grouping, the family: here some degree of control or influence
may be possible. Finally there are the individual stressors, pre-
dominantly based on changes in our life.

This last group of stressors is mainly responsible for stress-related
illnesses. This can be considered good news because it is this
group over which we have the greatest personal control. Even
happy changes, such as marriage, a new baby, or a promotion, can
produce stress. Bad changes are, of course, worse. In conjunction
with Richard Raahe, Thomas H. Holmes published a Social
Readjustment Rating Scale [*Volume 11, Journal of Psychosomatic
Research*, 1967]. This rated the following:

1. Death of spouse... 100
2. Divorce.. 73
3. Marital separation... 65
4. Prison term... 63
5. Death of a close family member.. 63
6. Personal injury or illness.. 53
7. Marriage.. 50
8. Being fired from work... 47
9. Marital reconciliation.. 45
10. Retirement... 45

11. Change in health of family member................................ 44
12. Pregnancy.. 40
13. Sexual difficulties... 39
14. Gain of new family member.. 39
15. Business readjustment.. 39
16. Change in financial state.. 38
17. Death of close friend.. 37
18. Change of occupation... 36
19. Increase in arguments with spouse.............................. 35
20. Mortgage or loan over £10,000.................................... 31
21. Foreclosure of mortgage or loan................................. 30
22. Change in work responsibilities.................................. 29
23. Son or daughter leaving home..................................... 29
24. Trouble with in-laws.. 29
25. Outstanding personal achievement.............................. 28
26. Spouse begins or stops work.. 26
27. Starting or finishing school... 26
28. Change in living conditions... 25
29. Revision of personal habits.. 24
30. Trouble with boss.. 23
31. Change in work hours or conditions............................ 20
32. Change in residence... 20
33. Change in schools... 20
34. Change in recreational habits...................................... 19
35. Change in religious activities....................................... 19
36. Change in social activities... 18
37. Mortgage or loan under £10,000.................................. 17
38. Change in sleeping habits.. 16
39. Change in number of family reunions......................... 15
40. Change in eating habits... 15
41. Vacation.. 13
42. Christmas.. 12
43. Minor violation of the law... 11

To find your score, it is suggested that you think back over the past year of your life and check any of the above events that have happened to you. Then add up the total points. According to the research findings, a score of 150 or more would give a 50/50 chance of developing an illness. A score of 300 or more would push that probability over 90 percent.

Having regard to the fact that the list was produced twenty years ago, it would probably be more valid to increase the mortgage amounts by a factor of five! There are also some notable absences from the list. For example, housework and shopping do not appear in it, but would almost certainly figure in the stress-promoting activities of some people.

It is interesting to note that the stresses include several items which are normally considered pleasurable, such as vacations and Christmas.

Stressbuster
**Close your eyes. Visualise a blackboard.
Imagine that the word "peace" is
being written on it in white chalk.
Breathe deeply.**

I could see peace instead of this

Some years ago my work took me [JS] to the industrial north-east of England and I spent most of my days amidst the smoke and fumes spewed out by the chimneys of innumerable steel works and chemical plants. One day I was visited by an artist friend, a painter, who deplored pollution and filth. I collected her from the railway station. It was early evening and the sun was low in the sky as we approached the factory complex which we had to pass on the way to my countryside home. The chimneys were still belching forth their vaporous fumes in shades of grey, red and yellow and I apologised for the "disgusting" sight. My friend, to my astonishment, expressed delight at the – to her artist's eyes – wondrous sight, heightened in its dramatic effect by the late sun's rays. What I had anticipated as distressful, she found to be eustressful: her perception of the environment was oblivious to the feelings of disgust which the view regularly produced in me.

A team of University of Chicago behavioural scientists some years ago carried out tests on the relationship between stress and illness and, amongst other findings, established that excessive stress experienced by two hundred executives at Illinois Bell Telephone Company at the time of a particularly stressful corporate situation had no significant effect on half of them. The other half became sick, but there was no way of correlating the sickness with the stress in the sense that the amount of stress, *per se*, was not the key to the subsequent state of health.

What was apparently true, however, was that there was a difference in reaction to the stressful events by those executives who remained healthy and those who became sick. The healthy managers regarded the situation as an inevitable part of corporate development, and tended to look at the positive features of the changing circumstances as an opportunity for growth and new experiences. They felt that they were in *control* of their personal situation and, even if they could not control the changes themselves, they could at least control their impact.

The healthy executives used "transformational coping" to deal with the situation. This involves "altering the events so they are less stressful. To do this, you must interact with the events and, by thinking about them optimistically and acting toward them decisively, change them in a less stressful direction." [Maddi, S.R. and Kobasa, S.C. *The Hardy Executive: Health Under Stress*, 1984, Homewood Il, Dow Jones-Irwin]. In contrast, the less healthy managers mostly used "regressive coping" which involves thinking about the events pessimistically and acting "evasively to avoid contact with them".

A fascinating experiment was described by J.V. Brady, "Ulcers in Executive Monkeys" [in *Scientific American*, 1958, 199 (4)m 95–100], whereby two monkeys were placed in adjacent cages in each of which a lever has been placed. One of the levers is effective, the other is not. If the effective lever is not pressed at least once every five seconds, both monkeys suffer an electric shock. Although both monkeys are identically affected by the shock, only one monkey (known as the executive monkey) has the power to control the electric shock and, by acting appropriately (i.e. pressing his lever at the appropriate intervals), to avoid the shocks.

The experiment was continued for some days, divided into six-hour work periods and six-hour rest periods. The monkey with the active lever learns to press it; the monkey with the "dummy" lever ultimately loses interest in it. Daily physiological tests fail to detect any abnormalities in either monkey. Both monkeys maintain a proper diet and weight.

Nevertheless after twenty days the executive monkey dies. The cause of death is ulcers. And, despite both monkeys having suffered identical shock experiences, the second monkey remained healthy. It was apparently having control, having to make the decisions, which was the critical factor in the stress.

An interesting parallel can be drawn here with a study carried out in Nebraska in 1978, which revealed that hypertension was four times more prevalent amongst air traffic controllers than air-crew. Diabetes and peptic ulcers were twice as high.

In another piece of research, involving lawyers, the behaviourists found that a commitment to their work and – once again – a sense of *control* determined the ability to cope with stressful situations without developing strain symptoms such as migraines, bad nerves, sleeplessness. The people suffering from these symptoms were those who had less belief in the importance of what they were doing, and less sense of direction.

If any conclusion is to be drawn from this research, therefore, it has to be that our physiological responses will be less intense if we regard stress as an inevitable part of life and a challenge rather than something which has to be avoided.

Case Study:

Mr. X has spent all his working life in the "stressful" conditions associated with city existence: noise, traffic, pollution, danger, hustle and bustle. By dint of hard work and careful financial husbandry, he is able to retire in his fifties. Finally he can fulfil his life's ambition: a country cottage far from the city's stress-laden strife. Six months later he moves back to the city. "I couldn't stand the silence," he confesses, "I was becoming stressed-out." He had moved from eustress to distress. It is easy (probably easier) to envisage someone born to country life, having precisely the same reaction after a move to the city. But in both cases the stress is within the person and not in their environment.

If we change ourselves, we change our world

All too often we respond not to the situations with which we are confronted, but to the interpretation we place on them. Or we anticipate problems and then, perversely, display anxiety when the situation does not produce the problems we had expected. We are stuck in a mental environment which does not match the world outside.

It is wise to start from the premise that the world about us is not going to change just because **we** *don't like it.*

Why should you change yourself?

Because *you* are the one suffering stress. *Your* body is paying the price. *You* are living at the dangerous edge.

Of course you have as much right as anyone else to suffer. It's your ulcer, your migraine, your divorce, your prescription, heart attack or heartache.

Once you realise that fact, and couple it with the assumption that things won't change because you want them to, you might start making a healthy change in your attitude to, and your relationship with, the world outside your skin.

We experience stress when we perceive a threat to ourselves or our situation in society, or when we believe we may have to face up to some radical pressure on our core values. When we cannot think of a way to change the perceived outside pressure, we become anxious. The anxiety results from the awareness of stress and the belief that we are unable to exert any effect on it. *If our external world is controlling our internal state we will, inevitably, be stressed.*

Now, what happens if we accept that we cannot change, or influence a change in, the external situation until we have started to change ourselves? This acceptance may help reduce the demands made upon our nervous system. This is a first step. The next step – a gigantic step – is to change our perception of the situation which has stressed us. And even though it is a "gigantic step", it is one which may be easier to take than you imagine.

Yes, there is a situation with which we are expected to cope. Yes, there is someone out there who expects something of us. But the stress we are experiencing and our anxiety exist only in our own mind. If, therefore, we change our perception by an act of simple reframing, we immediately change our perceived world. From this it is a small step to feeling relaxed rather than stressed.

And all that has really happened is that we have suddenly started looking somewhere else for our answers. We've stopped making the mistake of looking outside ourselves and have recognised that the answer is within.

we are stuck in
a mental environment
which does not match
the world outside

Assume that your boss is not going to get nicer, your children are not going to listen, your partner is not going to get a personality transplant, it won't be YOU who wins the lottery, your neighbours won't turn the volume down, the bills will still pour in.

You know that nothing has worked. You moaned, manoeuvred, pouted, pretended, complained, complied, whinged and wondered what it would take. You asked, answered back, joked and jockeyed for position. All to no avail, because THEY stay the same, the problems still loom large, the bullies still prevail. The world rolls on regardless.

Chapter Three

Using Stress Positively

One person's stress may be another person's stimulus

> ***Frustration is doing the same thing over and
> over and over, hoping for a different result***

Many of us, for most of our lives, have been waiting for permission to be ourselves. We have been approval-seekers. We have avoided action while waiting for validation. We have been fed – or have fed ourselves – a number of "should", "should not", "ought", and "ought not" messages. An instant antidote, is to change "should" to "could" and "ought not" to "why not?". This is the start of taking responsibility for ourselves, for our actions; this is the beginning of giving ourselves permission to be ourselves; this is the recognition that we have choice about our reactions to what happens in our lives. We can start taking some control. *We are less likely to be stressed when we feel in control of a situation.*

LESS LIKELY TO BE STRESSED WHEN WE FEEL IN CONTROL OF A SITUATION

A lot of stress results from repetitive actions, patterns of behaviour that are driven by habit and familiarity. Recognising these patterns gives us some opportunity to get off the treadmill, to change tack.

We structure time in order to get our needs met, whether through work, hobbies, solitude, ritual or intimacy.

"Games" are a way of getting close to people whilst simultaneously keeping our distance, or maintaining some reserve. Games which we are not aware of playing, end with familiar yet uncomfortable feelings. These feelings are the "payoff" which enable us to feel hard done by, or to justify dumping our feelings onto other people. We can convince ourselves that we are the injured party, or feel triumphant when we diminish others' sense of self.

Games are stressful. The effort of playing them puts enormous strain on our peace of mind and our physical well-being. The energy squandered could be better utilised in communicating more authentically, more openly and honestly; in short, more intimately.

Games are so named because they proceed according to certain (unwritten) rules. The players know what triggers the next stage, and the responses to each trigger. Games might also be considered a kind of dance, choreographed so that every player knows the proper steps and the exact sequence.

Because they are repetitive, games are predictable. This means we need not be surprised as each move in the dance, each gambit in the game, neatly unfolds. The Game Plan questionnaire on page 27 will help you to recognise the pattern so that you can, if you wish, do something to change the game, the dance.

The Game Plan is not about blaming, it is about taking responsibility for our own part in ongoing problems, and for doing something that makes a difference. If things are not as you would have them be, if you are feeling stressed, and if people won't change, one thing is clear: *you* must change!

You might ask, "Why should I be the one to change?" The answer is simple, though not easy: if you are the one suffering, and if what you are doing isn't working, do something different. If you are stuck in blaming and shaming, you may be denying your contribution to what is going on. The mother quoted in our case study on the next page needed to accept that her efforts were a futile waste of time, and worse. Her son wasn't listening, and she was feeling more and more powerless. She was losing her temper, her credibility, and any positive communication with her son.

It turned out that the son most vehemently rejected his mother's requests following visits to his father and his new partner. These visits stirred feelings of resentment, rejection and guilt in the mother, along with the need to maintain order in her own home. Her son, returning from his visits, needed to reflect on his hurt and loss, and wanted to curl up in front of the TV for a while. His mother would insist on the normal routine, say, eating together; her son would refuse.

Case Study:

It is important to understand the sequence of steps in a Game, but many players fail to recognise their own contribution to the process. The mother of a young man recently told me that her teenage son caused all the problems at home because, without provocation, he was disruptive, anti-social, and aggressive.

"How does it start?" I asked.
"He is just aggressive and unpleasant!"
"How, specifically, is he aggressive?"
"He's so rude."
"How is he rude?"
"He answers back and refuses to do things."

The son is answering back – which means it does not start with his answer! This mother is, understandably, focusing on what her son does, rather than what she can do differently.

The Game Plan helped the mother to see that she could respond differently; that they were getting locked into something unpleasant and unhealthy – a Game. From the boy's point of view, his mother seemed unsympathetic and uncaring, which discouraged him from talking to her.

Recognising the pattern, the mother was able to respond differently, which helped her son to change.

The Game Plan can be used before or after unpleasant – all too familiar – negative interactions.

To get a sense of how it might help to analyse what goes on, we suggest you think back over some recent unpleasant communications with people you know – friends, family or colleagues.

Later, you could use it to anticipate transactions that might go awry.

The Game Plan does not give answers; it simply helps you to become more aware and to take more responsibility for changing the process into something more constructive and less stressful.

Keeping an ongoing record will help you to track your development, and enable you to become more aware of the triggers that add to your stress. Use blank sheets of paper, or pages in your journal, to record your answers.

The Game Formula and the Game Plan

The Game Formula
Games have a formula, described by Eric Berne, the "father" of Transactional Analysis, as follows:

Con> Gimmick> Response> Switch> Crossup> Pay-Off

The first step is the Con, or Come-on. The basic message is: Do you want to play a Game in which we both get to feel stressed? The person being invited will respond with the Gimmick if s/he wants to feel the usual discomfort. If the Response indicates an affirmative *"Yes, I do want to play"*, the initiator responds in turn with another habitual, expected move. The next move is an internal Switch for both initiator and respondent. The respondent feels confused at this stage, and both players are left with stressed and stressful feelings. These are the Pay-offs that motivate the game.

Every time we initiate or acquiesce to a Game, we are, unconsciously, getting something – some Pay-off – from participating. At the very least we can go on pretending that we have no choice, or that we cannot change what we do – so we have to coerce or manipulate others to change what they do, or say, or feel.

The Game Plan
How does it start (What is the con or trigger)?
This could be a look, a tone of voice, the colour of an envelope, certain words, standing while the boss is sitting, sitting while the boss is standing.

Then what happens (What is the gimmick)?
You could smile when you feel insulted, stay silent when you need to speak, shout when you feel afraid, agree to "rescue"

someone to escape or avoid their displeasure or alleviate their distress (which adds to your own).

What happens next (How does the initiator respond to your gimmick)?
Do they raise their voice? Their eyebrows? The stakes? Does s/he become blubbery, belligerent, blaming or blameless? Do their responses stimulate guilt, shame or blame in you?

How does it end (What is the switch)?
Do either or both of you flounce off? Do you scream blue murder or have a tantrum?

What do you think when that happens (The crossup)?
What do you tell yourself about this interaction? Do you feel sorry for yourself, or hurt and misunderstood? Do you feel "got at", or determined to "get them back"?

How do you end up feeling (The pay-off)?
Sad? Mad? Scared? Glad? Triumphant? Overwhelmed? Undermined? Discounted? Disheartened? Disdainful? Distant?

Stressbuster
**Day-dream about your greatest achievement.
Breathe deeply.**

Chapter Four

Relaxation Techniques

Peace of mind is a piece of cake

Stressbuster
Remove your shoes and wiggle your toes.
Breathe deeply.

> # *Peace of mind is a piece of cake*

Relaxation is a rather loose term which can mean anything from just "taking things easy" to engaging in strenuous – albeit enjoyable – physical activities. The way in which we choose to use it in this book, is in the sense of releasing undesirable physical and mental tension through the *deliberate* action of "letting go".

It is ironic that so many people, who strive so hard to develop techniques for achieving their ambitions, fail to appreciate that it is equally important to learn techniques for relaxation. Many of them think they have merely to interrupt the activity which is producing tension or stress, and the undesirable by-products of this activity will disappear. This they regard as relaxation, little realising that – far too often – they continue to carry their stress and their worries around with them: on the golf course, at the card table, in front of the TV set.

All of which is not to say that there are no benefits to be obtained from a round of golf, a walk in the countryside, listening to music, etc., but those benefits can be enhanced considerably by the use of techniques for *conscious* relaxation, which will produce unimaginable advantages in the improved feeling of well-being and increased energy.

Conscious relaxation, using skills and methods taken from the various schools of meditation, can be easily learned and, once mastered, can be used regularly, whenever a few minutes are available during the working day, or for longer periods after work. They can be used to deal with body fatigue or mental languor; they can be used to dissipate feelings of frustration or anger, as, for example, when sitting at the wheel of a car in a traffic jam. They can be used to prepare the mind and body for a meeting or project which might otherwise be stress-inducing. They can be used as a healthy substitute for cigarettes or alcohol.

If we accept, as we must, that stress cannot be avoided, our aim should be to treat it positively, to get whatever benefit we can from it. There are a range of therapies, exercises and activities

31

which may be harnessed in order to achieve this aim. The purpose of this book is to help you to find your own most favourable methods towards your personal optimum stress level.

In this chapter we shall be describing some methods and offering some suggestions. They are by no means exhaustive.

Every day and in every way...

Studies of the effects of meditation have demonstrated that during the meditative state the heartbeat and the metabolic rate slow down, the body uses less oxygen, less carbon dioxide is produced, and a reduced state of tension is indicated. The meditation process has been shown to produce a physiological state of deep relaxation, of wakeful mental alertness, quite different from a hypnotic state and contrary to a state of anger and anxiety.

At its simplest level, therefore, meditation can be used to relax the mind and the body, to allow the mind to be stilled and serene, to combat stress, and to increase physical and mental energy. More deeply, meditation is used by its practitioners to achieve a state of bliss wherein they may understand the nature of consciousness and reality.

There are many different schools of meditation and the one which has received possibly the widest publicity in recent years is Transcendental Meditation (TM), but it is not the intention of the authors to support or recommend any particular method. There are, however, a number of common elements to any form of meditation, and the practice of these will undoubtedly be found beneficial in dealing with the stress in your life. Here, then, are some suggestions as to techniques and exercises which we have personally found helpful.

Ideally meditation should be performed in a quiet, warm place, free from interruptions. It may be performed either indoors or outside. Outdoor meditation can be very pleasant provided the right conditions of weather and surroundings can be found. This is not altogether an easy task in this day and age. It is also more effective if a particular time of day is set aside for the meditation, which need not occupy more than a minimum of ten or a maximum of thirty minutes. As with the physical yoga exercises in our next section, it is not recommended that you meditate immediately after meals. Meditation in the morning will help you to carry the serenity into your working day, but the time needed may be more difficult to find in the mornings. Meditation before bedtime could help you to sleep more soundly and more peaceably.

Meditation is best performed in a seated position and the yoga posture of *sukasana* (the easy posture) is the one which is usually favoured. This is a simple cross-legged position seated on the floor.

Those who find this cross-legged position difficult to adopt should sit in a comfortable straight-backed chair. The head and spine should be held straight and erect (a cushion can be placed against the small of the back to help keep it straight), and it helps to sit on a cushion or folded rug.

Probably the simplest of all meditation techniques involves merely breathing, where the breath is used as a focus for attention and a means of relaxing the body and calming the mind. When you are seated comfortably, close your eyes and start inhaling and expelling your breath completely. After two or three deep breaths, start counting the breaths on each out-breath. When you reach ten, start again with one. Don't worry if you lose count of the number, just start at one again. The object of the exercise is not to reach or control a particular number of breaths, but just to ensure awareness of your breathing. Practising this exercise for ten or fifteen minutes twice a day can be incredibly effective as a relax-ation technique. Don't worry about distractions, or the intrusion of stray thoughts, but gently turn your attention back to counting the breaths.

Another technique is to meditate with a *mantra*. A mantra is a special phrase which you repeat to yourself silently or out loud. According to the Yoga or Sufi mystical schools, the *vibrational qualities* of certain sounds is important to the effectiveness of the mantra. Many people, however, believe that any word or phrase will have the same effect. Or you could try thinking of an object, or an image, or a person, or a place that has pleasant connotations. One of the authors uses part of the old Coué phrase when he meditates: *Every day and in every way* [I'm getting better and better]. Close your eyes and visualise the image, object or place, or silently repeat the word or phrase to yourself. As with the breathing exercise, if you feel the outside world, or extraneous thoughts, intruding, ignore them and return to the meditation. Don't worry about the intrusion: this is quite normal. Practise this form of relaxation twice a day and amaze yourself at the benefit you will get from it.

Another form of unstructured meditation simply involves choosing a subject which has some significance to you and using it for the meditation. For example you might think about how you will achieve your full potential, or how you see yourself, or how you relate to others.

But whatever form of meditation you practise, it is important that you do it with patience and determination. If you maintain an open mind you will certainly make a number of unpredictable discoveries about yourself, and about the values you place on life.

Touches of sweet harmony

Yoga is a very practical way of dealing with the stressors of daily life and carries the added benefits of improving posture, reducing weight, and increasing energy and vitality. People who regularly practise only the more simple of yoga techniques are able to enjoy the mental tranquillity and emotional placidity which derive from them.

The stress of life doesn't merely affect the mind. Body and mind are interrelated, and whatever affects the mind will affect the body, just as whatever affects the body will affect the mind. Yoga techniques, which stretch, strengthen and improve the body, will also relax the mind and dissipate nervous tension.

Although there are several different systems of yoga, they all share the aim of relaxing and liberating the individual; of stilling the mind's ceaseless chatter; of transmitting tranquillity, serenity and joy. And the best part is the ease with which this can be practised and achieved, and the pleasure that it gives. No special equipment is needed: merely the time and the will to practise. There are no age barriers, nor are there any physical restrictions. Anyone can enjoy and profit from yoga.

It is not our intention to provide a yoga course within the confines of this book, or even to describe a series of exercises. There are numerous books on the shelves of your library or local bookshop, and there are a great many courses available if you wish to enjoy the benefits of yoga in more depth. But there is one simple technique which you can practise at any time, although it is not a good idea to practise it within two hours of having eaten, and that is the technique of *Uddiyana*, or the Abdominal Lift. The best times are first thing in the morning or before going to bed, and before breakfast, after a bowel movement, is probably the best time of all.

Uddiyana is practised in a standing position, with knees slightly bent as if you are about to squat, feet apart, toes straight ahead. The hands should be placed high up on the thighs with the fingers pointing inwards. You should then expel all air from the lungs; it is very important that this exhalation should be as complete as possible. Now the abdominal muscles should be pulled upwards and backwards towards the spine; a sort of "sucking" motion, rather as if you are trying to breathe deeply from the abdominal area, but without the air actually entering the lungs. This "abdominal lift" should be held for no more than three seconds and then the muscles relaxed. This entire movement should be repeated as often as possible between exhalations, but initially restrict yourself to no more than three. Five movements should be possible fairly quickly, and ultimately it may be possible to achieve between ten and twenty of them. Each set of movements is known as a round and a rest should be taken between rounds. Once again, start with three rounds and gradually work up to five. In due course you might want to perform even more, but for general health and relaxation, our recommendation would be to stop at five movements and five rounds, i.e. twenty-five movements in all.

35

The benefits of *Uddiyana* regularly practised will be felt in the stomach, colon, intestines, liver, kidneys, gall bladder, pancreas, and reproductive organs and glands. It helps to prevent constipation, reduces flabbiness in the waist and strengthens and improves the resilience of the abdominal muscles.

We hope that the practice of *Uddiyana* will encourage you to embark on, and benefit from, a yoga course where you will learn the *asanas* (postures). The most widely known of these are perhaps the lotus position, and the head and shoulder stands. But all the asanas are based on the same principle: that of stretching or extending the muscles without forcing or straining them. Over a period of time, practising these asanas will gradually lengthen the muscle fibres and make them more flexible. The muscular tone which the body develops aids mental relaxation and emotional tranquility. We then become calmer and find it easier to let go of stress and to handle stressors.

These physical techniques, particularly when taken in conjunction with the meditation described in the previous section, are amongst the most powerful tools at our disposal for the relief of tension and stress. However, for those readers who would prefer something even simpler, read on...

I think I can only manage 5 minutes on the nails.

Walk away from stress

Being healthy and fit may not remove the stressors from your life, but it cannot be denied that a fit and healthy body, which is host to a tranquil and serene mind, is a much better formula for keeping stress at bay, than a flabby mind in a flabby body. So how do you get the fit and healthy body? And how do you get and keep a fit and healthy mind?

Well, we've made a few suggestions in the earlier sections of this chapter, and we offer a few more in the later sections, but we have to confess that following any of these suggestions will require some effort and persistence, both to start and to maintain the disciplines of, for example, yoga, massage, meditation, aromatherapy, etc. In the meantime, what can you do that's easy, cheap, available, and requires little or no preparation?

The answer is: walk! Walk your way to fitness! Walk away from stress! All you need is a good pair of shoes.

This does not mean a five-minute stroll to the newsagents. Or ten minutes walking around the aisles of your local supermarket. Nor does it mean a one-hour leisurely walk, looking in shop windows during your lunchtime break from work. Walking, to do any real good, should be at a pace which will raise the pulse rate, exercise the lungs, and burn off the calories, and this means walking at a speed of at least 5 km or 3.5 miles per hour. Walk at the right speed, step out energetically, swing your arms, and you will exercise most of the muscles of your body.

It is true that a similar, possibly even more effective, amount of exercise could be achieved by cycling, or working-out, pumping iron, visiting your local gym, or swimming, but none of these can be undertaken with the same ease as walking. All you have to do is to substitute "Shanks's pony" for the car, the bus, or the train and you will be fitter, healthier, and less stressed.

The next time you are about to get into your car, ask yourself: "Can I walk there?" If not, perhaps you can park your car a mile or two from your destination and walk that mile or two. If you plan ahead, you could give yourself an extra fifteen or thirty minutes in order to accommodate a one- or two-mile walk. Do it often enough and – who knows? – you may end up enjoying it, even looking forward to it, and maybe planning longer walks when you don't have a specific destination.

Music hath charms

In June 1994, final-year undergraduate music student Ree Phillips of Kingston University completed a dissertation on *An Exploration of the Relationship between Music and Relaxation*. She came up with some very interesting findings, giving strength to the idea that music can have positive effects if used specifically for relaxation. In a questionnaire, she asked, *"Do you think that music can be used as an aid to relaxation?"*, to which ninety percent of respondents replied *"Yes"*. Another question was, *"If you were prescribed a piece of music by a doctor to listen to on a regular basis as an alternative to medication to aid relaxation, would you try it out?"* This time eighty percent of the sample replied in the affirmative, and it is clear that music is now generally believed to provide a form of complementary therapy in its own right.

Ree Phillips' research included a pilot study to measure people's heartbeat while they listened to various kinds of music. She found that music has a noticeable effect and that music intended for relaxation has a very positive effect. The graph below indicates the average heartbeat rate for those taking part in the study, measured first before any music was played, and then during the last ten minutes of each of eleven four-minute extracts. As can be seen, the heartbeat rate fell significantly during Albinoni's *Adagio*, and was also markedly lower during the performance of the relaxation pieces. In fact equal first place was shared by a Vivaldi adagietto and the title track from *Touching the Clouds* by Symbiosis.

Following Ree Phillips' research, music by Symbiosis was used in a study conducted by Saint Bartholomew's Hospital in London, where the beneficial effects of listening to *Touching the Clouds* was observed in patients with stress-related stomach problems.

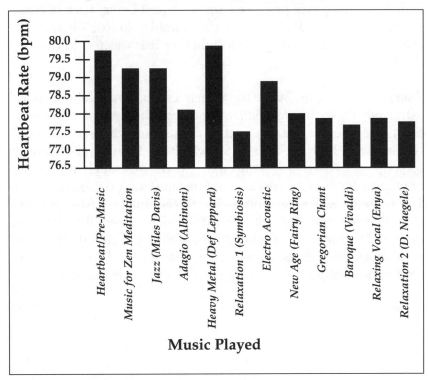

The sweet smell of successful stress relief

Aromatherapy is based on the use of natural essential oils extracted from herbs, flowers, fruit and trees. The oils, used in tiny quantities, provide a number of very useful tools for relaxing tension, reducing anxiety and relieving stress, and provide them in very pleasant ways. Whether the stressful state is a temporary one, such as regarding a pending interview, or a chronic condition, there is a range of essential oils which, added to a bath or compresses, massaged into the body, or inhaled, will stimulate, relax, soothe or calm as the situation requires.

Of the essential oils, lavender, mimosa, mandarin, neroli, patchouli, sandalwood and spruce are all calming oils; bergamot, frankincense, rosewood and violet are bracing; clary sage, jasmine and ylang-ylang will produce a sense of well-being. Each of these could be used individually or, preferably, in combination to combat stress, depending upon whether it is desired to calm or uplift.

There are three methods by which essences are obtained or extracted; these are *distillation, expression* and *solvent extraction*. Most true essences are obtained by distillation where the material is steamed at high pressure, after which the steam and vapour is cooled, condensed and collected. Citrus oils, such as lemon, orange and bergamot are obtained by squeezing (i.e. expression). The more expensive essential oils, those obtained from flowers such as roses and jasmine, are extracted by a lengthy chemical process in order not to damage the delicate material. Thus the basic essences such as lavender and tea-tree, and the citrus oils, tend to be considerably less expensive than the extractions.

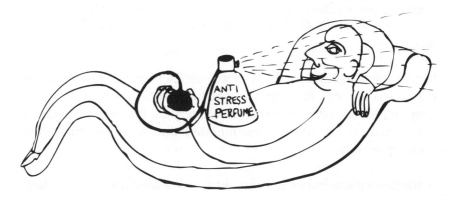

There is another important element in aromatherapy, and that is the use of a carrier or base oil to dilute the essential oils being employed. Generally only lavender and tea-tree are used undiluted in small quantities; all other essences must be diluted in a base oil. The best of these are obtained, as are the citrus oils, by expression, or *cold-pressing*. When purchasing these it is advisable to look for the use of the words *cold-pressed* or *virgin* on the labels, in order to ensure the highest quality.

Typical carrier or base oils would be avocado oil, almond oil, jojoba oil, or soya oil. This is not an exhaustive list and others such as grapeseed, sunflower seed and sesame seed also have their advocates.

There are many more oils than these, of course, and there are many books on your lending library shelves which will tell you how they may be best used to provide the desired relief or stimulation. Here, therefore, are just a few suggestions.

The use of lavender as a calming agent has long been known, and our great-grandmothers placed a few drops on their handkerchiefs, which they inhaled delicately to calm their nerves. The benefits have, however, been recognised since ancient Roman times when it was a favourite addition to the Roman bath. It is still useful for calming the nerves, and four or five drops in the bath will prove relaxing, particularly at night, either alone or in combination with other oils such as clary sage which has quite a bracing effect. And a few drops of lavender on a handkerchief, or as a cold compress across the forehead, is still a worthwhile exercise, particularly in dealing with a stress-related headache, where a sandalwood compress across the neck may also prove efficacious.

When using essential oils in direct contact with the skin, as in massage, they should never be used alone or in quantity, but as a drop or two added to the base (or carrier) oil. When used in combination, it is normally recommended that no more than five drops in total be used.

A fragrancer is another helpful aid to relaxation and stress relief. This is a bowl or pot which rests on a burner (using a small candle, such as a night-light) and which is filled with water to which a few drops of oil have been added. The candle beneath the bowl heats the water and slowly releases the fragrance of the oil into the air.

And, even more simply, you can buy candles already impregnated with essential oils as a way of fragrancing a room and as an aid to relaxation.

Eat, drink and be merry – for tomorrow you diet

This is in no way an attempt to suggest a diet, nor is it in any way an indication of the authors' eating patterns or beliefs; but the fact is that certain foods (in excess) "are bad for you", and certain foods are known to have a beneficial effect on health. It has been amply demonstrated that feelings of negative stress may be aggravated, if not caused, by eating habits. We have only to consider the clinical proof that certain "junk foods" have induced aggressive and hyperactive behaviour in children. It would seem appropriate, therefore, to list some of the factors which are regarded as contributory causes, and some of the recommendations for improvement.

An unhealthy diet, eating the wrong foods at irregular intervals, depriving the body of necessary vitamins and minerals, eating packaged and takeaway meals regularly rather than fresh foods, fruit, vegetables and salads will result ultimately in various physical symptoms. The skin will deteriorate in appearance, as will the hair; the teeth and gums will suffer; there may be a loss of energy; an incipient ulcer; difficulty in sleeping; some lethargy; and a tendency towards increased colds and illnesses.

This will not happen overnight, or even after a few weeks (say, after a holiday), but the effects are insidious and ultimately the body will suffer. Some deterioration of mental agility will occur along with potential harm to the nervous system.

Certainly anyone abusing their body in this way will suffer a discernible increase in negative stress.

As we have already said, it is not our intention to provide diet sheets and an eating plan, but here are some commonsense suggestions:

Foods which are bad for you (if eaten excessively):
    Sugar, salt and fats.
Foods which could be better:
    Pre-packaged foods, processed foods, foods high in preservatives and additives.

Foods which you are encouraged to eat:
> Fish rather than meat: grilled, steamed or baked rather than fried.
> Wholegrain cereals, wholemeal bread and pasta, brown rice.
> Honey in place of sugar.
> Fresh fruit, vegetables and salads.
> Low-fat dairy products such as cottage cheese and yoghurt.

You are also encouraged to reduce your intake of drinks with caffeine and to try to moderate your consumption of alcoholic beverages if you tend to drink more than, say, the equivalent of one pint of beer, a double whisky, or half a bottle of wine a day. Business lunches can be a source of over-indulgence!

THE AUTHORS ENJOYED RESEARCHING THIS SECTION (HIC!)

Chapter Five

Tips And Strategies

New age techniques for age-old conditions

> ### *Being OK can be stressful;*
> ### *being not-OK may be suicidal*

When faced by a stressful situation, the human body still responds in the same way as it responded in the time of the caveman facing the tiger in the undergrowth: the heart beats faster, the body tenses up, the breath becomes shallower and faster, the saliva dries up, the body sweats. This was fine when it was a necessary prerequisite to fight or flight. But if it is a reaction to the stress of modern-day life, with no opportunity to "let off steam" in a physical way, then the risk is run that the stress will cause health problems, such as high blood pressure, ulcers, hyper-ventilation, migraines, anxiety, insomnia, weight loss.

Analysis of any stressful situation will probably result in the discovery that it is self-perpetuating – that it is the result of a vicious circle. For example: (a) My son's behaviour upsets me – I feel guilty – my guilt makes me tense – I worry about it – I lie awake worrying about it – I get up feeling tired and irritable – I snap at my son – he gets upset – his behaviour then upsets me – I feel guilty… etc. (b) My boss complains about my performance – I feel anxious – my anxiety transmits itself to my clients – I lose orders – my boss complains about my performance. (c) My partner demands sex when I'm feeling too tired – I get nervous – my nervousness results in impotence – my partner becomes more demanding – my nervousness increases – I remain impotent – I become anxious – my partner demands sex… etc.

In order to avoid or moderate the physical and emotional side effects of stress, we tend to develop devices and strategies to provide immediate relief from these effects. We "blow our top", we act aggressively, we refuse to participate in stress-making activities. If we have a propensity to stress, however, these actions will only provide short-term relief – which is not to denigrate them, but clearly other measures are required to provide long-term benefits.

Psychoanalysis provides a number of useful descriptions of the types of defence we adopt in dealing with stress. *Repression* is one of the most powerful of these. We block from our awareness the stressful situation, thoughts, feelings or emotions. Another is *Displacement*, where we shift our feeling or activity into another channel or onto another person. *A Course in Miracles* has an excellent phrase for this: *I am never angry for the reason I think.* *Disavowal* or *Denial* is an extension of this ("I'm not going to continue this discussion."), particularly when combined with *Projection*: "I'm not angry, you are." "You're the one with the problem, not me!" This is often an indication of *Rationalisation*.

There are a vast number of psychotherapies and self-help systems on offer, many of which have borrowed and developed these concepts into a form which can be very useful in resolving stress patterns, and most of which will contain some form of recipe for recognising and combating negative stress. In choosing two or three of these to provide formulas for recognising negative stress symptoms, and strategies for combating them, we are not suggesting that there may not be other methods of achieving the same end results, but we have chosen those with which the authors are most familiar.

One such is Transactional Analysis (TA), and we have already introduced one of its concepts, the Game Plan, in Chapter Three.

Don't be fooled by the apparent simplicity of the ideas we've selected here. Although the concepts and techniques can be taught to young children, full understanding of their complexity requires in-depth study. We recommend that you explore some of the many TA books, courses and workshops available, but for our purposes we are outlining a few basic ideas to help you understand and reduce some of the stress you may be suffering. Furthermore, as well as helping you understand what, in the here and now and in your personal history, triggers stress, TA can help preclude future stress reactions.

TA is a model of personal and interpersonal relationships developed in the 1960s by Eric Berne. In providing frameworks for analysing thinking and feeling processes, and the transactions that occur between people, TA helps describe and make sense of how and why people do what they do.

First, a brief overview of some important TA concepts. As children, we spend our time learning how to adapt to the infinitely varied, utterly fascinating, incredibly frustrating, and totally strange world into which we emerge. Because we want and need to belong, we WANT to learn the rules, even if we have no idea that rules exist.

Powerful others, parents in particular, and grown-ups in general, with the best of intentions attempt to teach us how to "fit in", how to survive and (hopefully) thrive. We come to realise that love is, or will quickly become, conditional.

Parents usually want the best for us. They do the best they can on our behalf, but they, too, are conditioned by their history and upbringing. From the perspective of their cultural norms and standards, adults act and express feelings and say things which children try to evaluate, emulate, or perhaps escape from.

Our parents, and other important people who influence our upbringing by example and exhortation, encourage our beliefs and behaviour. We, perforce, either comply with or rebel against them. They may teach us the value of Determination and Persistence, in pursuit of Achievement and Success. Perhaps they encourage or admonish us to treat others with Kindness and Consideration, or to respond to tribulations with Courage and Strength. We may learn to prize Diligence, Industry and Efficiency above all else.

You probably know, or can figure out, which of the above values your parents held dear. You may at times have railed against your parents' values or, like many others, find that those values have a powerful and tenacious influence on your reactions and responses to people and events.

Most people tend, sooner or later, to internalise their parents' rules and standards, and translate them into values for living. It is as if a parent has taken up permanent residence in the back of the mind. This Ego State, the internal Parent, whether Critical or Nurturing, sets up a dialogue with an internal Child Ego State. To differentiate them from the "real thing", the Ego States (Parent, Adult, Child) are initialised with capital letters.

Whilst a lot of positive and necessary outcomes follow from the interaction between these Ego States, so does a great deal of stress and distress. Imagine that the inner Parent and Child Ego States are continuing the process that goes on in any normal relationship between parents and children. A youngster, hearing and observing rules for living, and doing his or her best to fit in, may come to the decision that s/he must strive to be and do something more than the basic values we have already mentioned.

They may conclude that Determination and Persistence involve never being satisfied, never relaxing. The person chasing Achievement and Success may be overly anxious about making a mistake, or even taking calculated risks. Somebody who wants to be Kind and Considerate may feel unable to be assertive or to ask for their own needs to be met. This could make it impossible for them to refuse requests, thus adding to pressure and stress.

Courage and Strength may be translated into a rule to hide feelings, never give up, admit vulnerability or ask for help. Diligence, Industry and Efficiency may result in the person never having time to think or relax.

To emphasise the point, the values are constructive and positive, but they may be internalised as "injunctions".

Injunctions – the "Don't" messages between the Parent and Child Ego States – solidify into six powerful messages that compel behaviour patterns and drive us to behave in certain ways. These *Drivers* are Try Hard, Hurry Up, Be Perfect, Be Strong, Please Me, Please You. We all have all of the Drivers, with one or two predominating. Any of them, separately or in combination, can push us towards stressful patterns of feeling, thinking and doing. These patterns are legacies of childhood, and often keep us hooked into childlike relationships with other people based on dependency and feelings inappropriate to mature adulthood. Drivers are the first step in the games people play.

Drivers

Perfection
Many of us strive to achieve success at work and at home. We want our voice to be heard, our hopes and aspirations valued and

validated, and our sense of self to be respected. Many of us would also like to achieve some degree of autonomy in our dealings with people and situations.

The need to be seen as or the desire to *BE PERFECT* can prevent people acting in a natural, relaxed manner. Driven with the need for perfection, we worry about making mistakes or taking risks. Fear of inefficiency can create or increase stressful feelings and drive us beyond reason to avoid mistakes at all costs. Excessive stress is too high a cost!

Pleasing

It is good and healthy to give and share pleasure with people, to treat people who are close to us with the same kindness and consideration we tend to show complete strangers. It is loving and supportive to give help and advice when it is requested or essential for people's growth and development – whether personal or professional. To give good service at work is not only behaving with integrity, it helps make the day's work more enjoyable. These attitudes and intentions generate good feelings and help build good relationships.

When, however, in an attempt to *PLEASE OTHERS* we take these sentiments too far, we may never be able to refuse a request or say "No!" We won't ask for our own needs to be met or acknowledged. Fear of being criticised, rejected or left in the cold may prevent us from asserting ourselves even when necessary and appropriate.

Strength

There are many situations in which we need to act courageously. People at work and at home need to know that they can rely on us, that we won't break under *appropriate* pressure. We need strength of character to face the day-to-day challenges that life throws our way, and to recognise the incredible resourcefulness and resilience that we have.

When these values become compelling, when they drive us beyond logic or reason, we may start hiding ordinary human feelings. This prevents us asking for help or support. We become afraid of being seen as helpless or inadequate by "giving in", then doubly afraid of the fear itself being exposed. In the struggle to *BE STRONG*, we build walls of silence and isolation. These walls create prisons of loneliness, and yet more fear of exposure. The pressure to cope, to manage, to survive the pressure become a treadmill, a rut, an endless loop or groove that keeps us running around in circles. We can end up spiralling out of control, and it can kill us.

Trying

To persist in a determined and, if necessary, patient manner helps us to achieve many of the goals we set ourselves. It is healthy and wise to give the appropriate effort and energy to our chosen or designated tasks. It is honourable to be diligently industrious to complete what we set out to achieve in a day or a life. If perseverance and persistence become obsessive, if our determination becomes unreasonable, we may push on, never satisfied, never resting or relaxing. When we are driven by pride or pretension to *TRY HARD* because we fear failure, we may become workaholics who are dulled and deadened beyond prudence or practicality.

Hurrying

We can be driven to *HURRY UP* to such an extent that the clock rules our lives. We stop being efficient in our time management strategies. It makes sense to be efficient and respond without undue haste in order to meet timetables, deadlines, commitments or appointments. This "Driver" makes time management highly stressful and can impair our ability to think, to relax, to take the time and find the balance we need to live lives that have the optimum, rather than the maximum, stress levels.

Understanding your own Drivers enables you to begin making different choices about how you respond to different triggers. The following questionnaire will give you some understanding of your own Drivers. Simply give a value of 1 (I do not resonate greatly with this), 2 (this produces an echo in me), or 3 (yes, I identify with this), then total them at the end.

Please (others)

I don't like people leaving me on my own ( )
I try to look pleased when I'm talking to someone ( )
I'd rather put off unpleasantness ( )
I say "y'know" and nod a lot in conversation ( )
I show my uniqueness by the way I dress ( )
I laugh or giggle when I feel anxious ( )
I "sugar-coat" any requests I may make ( )
I hide my tears behind a smile ( )
I let others go first ( )
I can get agitated when I'm on my own ( )

TOTAL ( )

Be Perfect

Being criticised makes me feel I am not respected ( )
I ask people to explain or justify their mistakes ( )
I prefer to be on time or even early ( )
I like to see and keep things neat and tidy ( )
I tend to walk and sit with an upright posture ( )
I readily judge and criticise other people ( )
I gather interesting facts or information ( )
I focus a lot on details ( )
I like things to be just as they should be ( )
If I want something done, it's better to do it myself ( )

TOTAL ( )

Try Hard

I don't like things being wrong or unfinished ( )
I tend to start but not finish things ( )
I realise (too late) there was an easier way ( )
I'm sure (often wrongly) I'll get it right THIS time ( )
I can feel envious when others get things right ( )
I prevaricate over important things ( )
I get close to completion and give up ( )
I can be totally disorganised ( )
I am often late ( )
I often don't start at all ( )

TOTAL ( )

Hurry Up

I don't like being delayed or wasting time	( )
I make haste when it isn't strictly necessary	( )
I fail to shop for necessities	( )
I can get agitated when it's time to get going	( )
I drum my fingers, wriggle my feet, jiggle my knees	( )
I take on too much, then rush things	( )
I can be clumsy	( )
I "push" people to get them to speed things up	( )
I "march" whilst waiting	( )
I walk, talk, eat, live fast	( )

TOTAL   ( )

Be Strong

I think that being reliant on others is "weak"	( )
I play things cool, even if I'm upset	( )
I ponder long and hard before committing myself	( )
I plan to make sacrifices	( )
I load myself with things I don't need	( )
I put up with more (and for longer) than I need to	( )
I "rescue" people by doing things they could do for themselves	( )
I take great caution	( )
I wear a mask to cover emotions	( )
I may not notice what's happening in my body	( )

TOTAL   ( )

Dealing With Drivers
(Giving yourself permission)

Hurry Up

Give yourself permission to be late. Tell yourself that nobody expects you to be dead on time. Try making "imprecise" appointments. "I'll see you around 10am." instead of "I'll see you at 10am." Since Hurry Up is identified with "rushing in where angels fear to tread", you need to prepare for tasks and activities; plan them in advance; listen to people instead of thinking about how you are going to interrupt them while they are speaking.

Please

Give yourself permission to consider your own needs before those of others. Learn how to say "no" assertively but gracefully. If you never say no, you are ultimately unlikely to be believed whenever you say yes. You will get a reputation for unreliability; for lying at worst, for being a romancer at best.

Be Perfect

Give yourself permission to laugh at yourself. Accept that you can make mistakes and teach yourself to acknowledge that it's OK to do so. You are, after all, no less human than the next person.

Try Hard

Treat all problems as challenges or opportunities. Try to avoid getting bored with things you've started doing. Treat all changes as challenges. Put a double-ell-ee into change to produce challenge. Recognise that "nothing is static but change" and don't be taken by surprise when changes occur.

Give yourself permission to do what you want to do rather than what you think you ought to do.

Be Strong

Don't be afraid to show your feelings. Hiding or disguising your feelings can produce stress. Allowing people to know how you feel is a way of relieving that stress.

Give yourself permission to ask for help. Don't be afraid or reluctant to cry. One of the difficulties many men (in particular) experience when studying co-counselling (and I was one of them!) is to learn to aid the catharsis of discharge by crying freely. It was hard to forget the childhood taunts of "cry-baby".

Give yourself permission to accept the gifts offered by others.

Chapter Six

Taking Charge

Do I want justice, or do I want tranquillity?

Stressbuster
Focus all your attention on a single object.
Think about its shape, its texture and breathe deeply.

> ***Just because things are different
> doesn't mean they have changed***

Life makes many demands on us, to which we must respond. Our choices of response are fairly limited in number. We can ignore the stimulus, fight or flee, or go with the flow, i.e. manage the situation, the relationship, our lives. We will either want to change things, reactively or creatively, or attempt to prevent change, either passively or aggressively.

When forced to respond to life's stressors, we experience stress reactions either in the head, the heart or the gut. In other words, we respond either mentally (psychologically), emotionally or physically.

Emotional responses are to do with feelings, of course, but we often ignore this simple and sometimes dangerous truth. Stress Kills – so take charge of your emotional reactions to people and events!

Psychological responses may impair your ability to think or function like intelligent people who can solve their own problems. When this happens you may overreact emotionally rather than rationally and appropriately (which is not to deny the appropriateness of feelings and emotions).

Physical reactions could be expressed through stress-related or stress-triggered illnesses and ailments.

An emotional reaction may be a feeling of depression or anger; psychologically we may have nagging doubts or "crazy" thoughts; physical symptoms may be anything from a nagging headache to a lethal heart attack.

Any and all of these will impact on our relationships, our social self, our very sense of self; our identity. Many people, unduly stressed, don't know where they are, where they're going, who they can turn to or even who they are.

The degree of stress will depend partly on what we tell ourselves about our ability to meet the demands made on our internal and external resources. It will be more stressful if the imbalance between demand and capability is too great.

More often than you might imagine, internal dialogue, or "self talk," serves to convince us that we are less able, less resourceful than we really are. Negative self-talk can be a hard taskmaster, driving us to distraction or distress, taking the wind out of our sails, or pushing us to go beyond the call of reason or duty in an effort to quieten the inner clamour. Much of the time, because it is so familiar, because the habit is so strong, we are not even aware of our self-talk. If we do not know that we are running an internal dialogue or monologue, we can do little to take control of our inner processes.

This inner voice can be positive or negative, supportive and discouraging, benign or baleful. It can be very helpful to start listening to these voices. Tuning in to them does not mean that you are "hearing things". It means paying attention to the messages you give yourself when approaching challenge and change. It means listening to the thoughts that disrupt your focus of attention or your peace of mind.

Stop right now and begin listening to the thoughts you have about your physical being. What do you say to yourself about your feelings, or other people's feelings?

What messages do you have in your mind about certain behaviours, actions or reactions? What do you think about pressure itself? Or about stress?

Some people thrive on pressure, saying it helps them to achieve their goals. You could be one such person. You may react to pressure by saying to yourself, "Why me?" or, "Poor me!"

The head and the heart, our feelings and thoughts, are inextricably linked.

Thoughts have a direct physical effect on what happens in the body. The effects include chemical and other changes and the output or suppression of various substances into the body and blood-stream.

Our feelings impact on our thoughts: a tensing of the stomach, a sudden lurch of the heart, will transmit messages which the brain must decipher, interpret, make decisions about, act upon.

Understanding this connection will help you to (re)gain control over your internal processes and your external behaviours.

The internal processes are always happening in the present. You may remember feelings or anticipate them, but, unless you are having the same feeling NOW, a memory or a fear is not a feeling.

For example, I think about a meeting I must attend, knowing that Fred will be there. I am still angry whenever I think about something Fred said or did last week. If I don't think about it, I don't feel angry, but the scheduled meeting is causing me some anxiety: what if I blow my top?

In such a situation the worry is happening now, but it is about something that has not yet occurred and the anger that I feel may not be anywhere near the surface (unless I think about it).

The present moment is a link between the past and the future. Much of what we think right now (and when else is there?) is shaped and moulded by our past, just as much of what we worry about is being forged in the fire of the present moment.

> ***Discard expectations; embrace experiences***

Handling Stress In Relationships

Here are some techniques for improving stressful situations in personal relationships and for setting a more realistic pattern for greater harmony.

- Discard all unrealistic expectations.

- Accept responsibility for yourself. Do not dump your responsibility on the other person.
- Make sure you are communicating an unadulterated message, and receiving the message the other person is wanting to send rather than the one you would prefer to hear. Train yourself to recognise the difference between the two.

- Don't play games. Be authentic.
- Consider positive aspects of the relationship; minimise the negative aspects. If the negative aspects continue to outweigh the positive features of the relationship, think seriously about the possibility that the best solution might be to end the relationship.
- Acknowledge the other person's positive qualities, first in your own mind, and then validate them directly to the other person.
- When it becomes necessary to have a serious discussion about terminating the relationship, do not blame the other person or yourself. Be assertive but not aggressive.

Try the following joint exercise.

Each of you writes down on a sheet (or sheets) of paper the answers to the following questions:

1. What do I need for it to work?

2. What are my hopes, fears, aspirations and needs generally?
3. What is the bottom line? What is the minimum requirement for an ongoing relationship? What would I find intolerable, i.e. the "unacceptable face of the relationship" which could spell the end?
4. What do I do if my needs are not met?
5. What will I have to give up? What am I prepared to give up?
6. What are my options?
7. Could there be other options that I have not considered?
8. Appreciations! *[This is probably the most important item in the list. No matter how critical you may feel of the other person, it is essential that you recognise and appreciate those positive qualities which they possess – after all, they are probably what attracted you in the first place!]*

Then, together, read, compare and discuss the answers to each question in a calm and positive manner, respecting and honouring the other person's right to their own beliefs, their own feelings, and their own statements. Regardless of the outcome of the exercise, you end it by expressing your appreciation of the other person's courage and honesty in participating.

> ### You scratch my back, and I'll scratch yours

Co-counselling and Stress Management

Just as with the techniques in Chapter Five derived from Transactional Analysis, the authors would recommend a deeper study of Co-counselling which requires participation in a basic training course (often called Fundamentals). Details of available courses are provided in an appendix.

But, as with the other sections, we are able to suggest techniques based on the principles of co-counselling which will be beneficial in handling situations of negative stress and, indeed, may be found useful in many other contexts.

What is Co-counselling?

It is a self-help therapy whereby we are able to exercise more control over our lives. A study of co-counselling involves recognition of our feelings and the influence they have on our lives. We then work on ways of changing these influences by various methods. These methods normally involve two people – the *Client* and the *Counsellor* – who make a *Contract* for a particular *Session*. The fact that only two people are needed for a co-counselling session makes it one of the most available forms of self-help therapy.

There are five main principles which are fundamental to the practice of co-counselling:

1. Total confidentiality as to time, place and people
2. Client is always in charge
3. Time is divided equally between Client and Counsellor
4. Equality and reciprocity exist between Client and Counsellor
5. Contracts are strictly enforced

Item 1 is self-explanatory, but for a trained Co-counsellor it is so important that Counsellor is frequently unable to remember Client's material at a subsequent session, because they have learned to "put it out of their mind" immediately the session has ended.

Item 2 means that in co-counselling – unlike other forms of coun-selling – Client establishes the ground rules and Counsellor is not permitted to deviate from them. This, as well as Item 5, is described below.

In co-counselling, after a session has been completed, the roles are reversed (Client becomes Counsellor and *vice versa*), and whatever time was given to Client is now given to Counsellor (become Client), and whatever contracts were made between them in the original roles are duplicated in the reversed roles. The original Counsellor in the role of Client may use the time for whatever purpose they desire: to discharge feelings of their own – whether stressful or not – or even to celebrate joyful feelings. We would suggest, however, that in the case of practitioners who are not qualified Co-counsellors, Items 3 and 4 may be disregarded.

Forms of Contract
In co-counselling there are three basic forms of contract:

(a) Free attention, whereby Counsellor gives no feedback at all to Client, but gives total, distress-free, unemotional and expres-sionless attention to Client, maintaining eye contact through-out. This can be difficult to achieve without training and is not the recommended contract for unqualified Co-counsellors.
(b) Intensive, which is a form of contract which should only be attempted by fully-qualified Co-counsellors.
(c) Normal, where prescribed interventions are given, and some suggestions are made as to the process of the Session. This is the type of Contract on which exercises may be attempted by unqualified practitioners with some benefit, and will form the basis of our suggested techniques in the remainder of this section.

Methods of Working
Starting a Co-counselling Session
It is recommended that a firm time is fixed for the length of the session, and "counsellor" is responsible for time-keeping. It should also be established whether or not counsellor will want to have equal time as client afterwards. Client should tell counsellor how much warning time is required before the end of the session, for example five minutes.

Working in a Co-counselling Session

It is useful to start with some "loosening" exercises. Client might do some gentle physical exercises, flexing muscles, stretching, etc. Exaggerated yawning is a good loosener. If client knows what it is hoped to achieve, what problem is to be solved, or what insight is desired, this may be established and some of the techniques described below may be adopted by counsellor if deviation from the specified aim is suspected.

Ending a Co-counselling Session

Counsellor to warn client that end of session is approaching (e.g. five-minute warning). Client may use this time profitably to establish what has been achieved and to think of a way of reinforcing what has been learned. Before the session ends, and certainly before an exchange of roles if that is intended, counsellor should make absolutely sure that client is no longer involved in his/her material. There are a number of ways this can be done, and these are suggested in the techniques described below.

Techniques of Co-counselling

The Hug

It has become customary for client and counsellor to hug before and after a session. This is really to establish the four pillars on which a co-counselling contract is built: security, safety, trust and confidentiality before the session, and to affirm and reinforce these at the end of the session, as well as expressing appreciation for the sharing.

The Personal Pronoun and the Present Tense

It has been found that co-counselling is more effective when client uses only the first person singular and the present tense.

For a co-counselling session to be effective it is essential that nothing is offered by counsellor which has not been requested by client; that no advice, opinions, sympathy, criticism or interpretations be offered during or after the time client is working; and that attention is maintained by counsellor throughout.

Interventions may be made, in a prescribed form, if at any time counsellor feels that client is "stuck", deviating from the desired aim, or avoiding an issue. Such interventions are effective in removing blockages and may take the form of:

Repetition
Counsellor asks client to "say it again"; several times if necessary.

Emphasis
Counsellor asks client to "say it louder", "make a movement stronger".

Role-playing, Role-switching
Counsellor asks client to take the position of another party, such as "What might they be saying?"; "What would you say if the roles were reversed?"

Contradiction
Counsellor asks client to "contradict that last remark".

Reminder of Responsibility and Tense
Client is asked to "put that into the present tense," or "put that into the first person". Using the pronoun "you" or "one" is a way of avoiding taking personal responsibility.

When client has completed his/her session, there are two further strategies which are useful:

Goal Setting
Here client sets goals as a way of establishing priorities for the future and this can be followed by:

Action Planning
Where counsellor will ask some or all of the following questions of client:

- What do you want?
- How will you know when you have it?
- What is the first step?
- When will you do it?
- Who will you talk to?
- What will you do/say?
- What might stop you? (How might you stop yourself?)
- How can you overcome that?

Finally

No (one-way) session is completed until counsellor is completely satisfied that client is no longer involved in his/her material, but has returned to, and has full attention in, present time. This can be achieved by various simple exercises which involve client's attention being fully engaged in present time. A fairly regular method is to ask client to name (say) five red (or blue, or any other colour) things in the room. Client might be asked to name five authors, actors, countries, plays, etc., which begin with a particular letter. Only after counsellor is convinced the client is orientated in the present may roles be switched.

Chapter Seven

Dying For Work

If work is a drug, kick the habit

If work is a drug, kick the habit

It was as recently as 1995 that the Health and Safety Executive recommended that employers should take reasonable steps to ensure the psychological as well as the physical well-being of their workers. In a well-reported case brought against a county council by a social worker, the council was found liable for one of the worker's two nervous breakdowns caused by work overload and was obliged to pay a very large sum in damages.

Now, while in no way wishing to suggest that employers do not bear a responsibility for the health and welfare of their workers, we would deplore any statement which detracts from the individual's own responsibility to protect his or her mind and body. In a society which tends more and more to deny personal responsibility, our aim is to define and describe those steps which we can – indeed must – take to enhance our lives.

Let us start with a straightforward acknowledgment: life is often stressful, and working life is more pressured and may be more stressful than ever before.

Now, in what way does stress at work resemble, and in what way might it differ from, the general considerations which we have discussed so far in this book?

It may be helpful first to summarise some of the points we have already made. What is stress? Basically it is a message from the body letting us know that demands are being made on our system. These demands may stem from changes on the outside or perceptions on the inside. The pressures may stimulate and motivate, or sap our energy and enthusiasm.

The problem is not, in and of itself, stress; stress can be either positive or negative. Stress is inevitable and, to a degree, necessary – even desirable. What might make it a problem would be the amount, extent, degree, and impact of negative stress on our hearts, minds, bodies and relationships.

The effects of stress are as varied as the causes. Some people are motivated or spurred on by stress. Actors who suffer first-night nerves may give the performance of their lives. Athletes may break records, authors achieve new prosaic heights. Without a certain amount of stress these people may fall far short of their potential; spurred on by it, they may reach the stars.

Some of the negative effects of stress are life-threatening. Whilst some people reach for the stars, others are digging themselves an early grave.

When the world is causing you stress, and the world won't change, a simple fact follows – YOU must change!

You may think this is unfair, unjust, unreasonable, impractical or impossible. Perhaps. But consider: if you are the one suffering stress, and the causes of stress are utterly beyond your control, *your* body pays the price, *your* mind gets lost in confusion, *your* spirit is daunted, *your* relationships explode into aggression or violation, or wither and die leaving nothing but the ashes of dead hopes and the shards of broken dreams.

Change of mind, change of heart

This book is about taking responsibility for your own state of mind, your physical well-being, the day-to-day business of inter-personal transactions, the shape of your future and the quality of your life.

Before moving on to explore these issues in greater detail and sug-gesting simple strategies and techniques for reducing stress in your life, we want to place everything in a moral context.

We are very aware of the moral or ethical perspective of stressful workplaces and relationships. There are environments, actions and reactions that are both illegal and immoral. It is a simple and sad reality that many bosses are insecure bullies and tyrants who exploit, mistreat or abuse their subordinates. Some are blatant, others are covert and cowardly.

The latter are usually aware of what they are doing, the former may not be. There are ways of responding to both.

It is equally true that many workplaces are pressurised hothouses of demands and tensions driven only by the need to prevail in the marketplace – profit at any cost, and, all too often, the human cost is ignored in the equation.

> *A high standard of living and a good quality*
> *of life are not necessarily the same thing*

If you are part of that human cost, and if "they" don't care, *you* must. You must start looking after yourself. Shift the focus from blaming them to taking responsibility for yourself.

Many managers have non-effective or virtually non-existent communication or listening skills. They lack empathy, or lack the courage or compassion to express sympathy. Their inability to recognise another point of view, let alone validate it, does not bode well for their rapport-building skills. They can seldom predict, let alone prevent, personnel problems and personality clashes. Ironically, if they don't actually cause these problems, they certainly exacerbate them.

If your work or workplace is causing you pain and distress, you have various options. We recognise that having options does not mean that you necessarily have easy choices. Your choices may lie between the Devil and the Deep, between Hell and Purgatory, between the fire and the fryer; but never believe you have *no* choice.

We may have to choose between bad health and a lower standard of living, between doing the job we studied, trained and aimed for, or a less stressful job that allows time and energy to play with our children or relax with family and friends. Given the choice between pleasing their boss and losing their partner, many choose the former. What price a soul?

We can stay in the situation and stay stressed, or opt to move on (get a new job) or move up or down (get a new position). We may (if health allows) keep the job whilst trying to change the environment or the relationships. We can stay, accept what cannot be changed, and change the way we react to it. And there are other options.

You ALWAYS have choice; even believing you have no choice is a choice in itself.

Everything you do is a choice, albeit forced upon you. Failure to recognise this may prevent you from grasping one of the most straightforward concepts in stress reduction.

> *A first step in reducing or removing stress in your work and life is to change the way you perceive or interpret what happens in your relationships at work*

This does NOT mean letting other people get away with unreasonable and unacceptable and, as likely as not, unlawful behaviour. Indeed, a great deal of stress results from exactly that: letting people get away with oppressive, disrespectful, bullying behaviour for the simple reason that they are slightly higher up the ladder in the hierarchy.

We accept that the choices available may seem to be no choice at all – but you *always* have choice. You can say nothing, but seethe inside. You can whinge, but never talk *to* those who "persecute" you. You can choose to stay quiet because you are able to maintain an inner tranquillity, to be your own centre of gravity. And you can learn techniques, develop skills for "caringly confronting" those who mistreat or torment you. There are countless ways of taking charge of your internal state and, hopefully, having more influence over your external circumstances.

The world is not necessarily the way you experience it. Your experience is valid, although even the validity of your experience can be questioned. There may be a gap between your perception and what *actually* happened. "The truth," said Oscar Wilde, "is rarely pure and never simple!"

Your "map" of events may not be an exact representation of what is or was going on. Current and recollected experiences are "filtered" through our feelings, prejudices, beliefs and values. We chisel and change things to suit our dreams or disappointments, to enlarge our fears, fantasies and failings.

One person's stressful and debilitating workload is another's challenge to succeed and excel. An imminent appraisal meeting may, for one employee, be a cause of soul-shrivelling dread, whilst a colleague may approach it as an opportunity to grow and develop.

Furthermore, stress relates not only to *what* happens, but where and when the event occurs. Time and place can contribute as much to stress as people and pressure. If you know, or can ascertain, in what circumstances, location, or context stress is triggered or intensified, you have more likelihood of changing the situation. At the very least you can be better prepared for your reactions to the stressors.

Stress also tends to be more prevalent at certain given times. Monday mornings and Friday afternoons are usually the most stressful times at work, as well as being the times when heart attacks are most likely.

If you keep a stress logbook, you could take note of recurrent stressful feelings, and their triggers, and could record, at least roughly, the time of day and the place they occur.

You might then well begin to notice a pattern: every Monday morning and Friday afternoon, for example; greater anxiety if you are summoned to the boss's office or, conversely, when the boss enters your domain, or when you are sitting and the boss is standing, or *vice versa*.

...or, perhaps when you have rushed out of the house without your usual breakfast, or mid-afternoon when you have, yet again, not allowed time for some lunch (and digesting it!).

It has been suggested that there are two types of personality in the workplace who are most at risk from stress:

Type A are those who claim to thrive on stress. Into this category come workaholics. Type A people tend to produce high levels of noradrenalin in their bodies, which acts like some drugs in inducing confidence and good feelings. Such people, however, can become addicted to these feelings (the workaholics, for example) and they then run similar risks to those associated with other types of addiction.

Type B, the overachievers, are the other type of person at risk. They set high standards (the TRY HARDER and BE PERFECT types described in Chapter Five), often have careers in the caring professions, and tend to expect others to reach the same high standards as they set themselves.

Some of the major causes of stress for these types might be:

- Ambiguity over job priorities
- Confusion over their role
- Uncertainty over their position in the managerial hierarchy
- Doubts about their competence
- Frustrations in decision-making
- Perceived job insecurity or lack of anticipated promotional prospects
- Inability to identify the demands of superiors satisfactorily
- Lack of communication with superiors and colleagues
- A perceived lack of cooperation by fellow workers

Having dealt with theory, let's give some practical workplace examples and offer some practical advice.

Here are some typical workplace stressors. How many of them apply to you?

- Too many distractions; insufficient time

- Lack of support from superiors; lack of effectiveness from subordinates
- Too many demands on competence, ability, time
- Having to work to deadlines
- Inability to delegate, or lack of trust/confidence in delegatee
- Physically inadequate, unpleasant, uncomfortable working conditions
- Having to learn new skills
- Increasing age without improvement in seniority. Concern that junior staff may try to sabotage you. Office politics
- Interference with family life

Now ask yourself how many of the above might be viewed as challenges rather than anxiety-making problems.

When viewed as a challenge how would each "problem" be handled?

Which of the following do you find particularly stressful?

- Having too much work
- Being a slave to addictive behaviour patterns and unhealthy dependence on alcohol, cigarettes, drugs
- Having to work to time constraints
- Having to spend too much time travelling to/from/during work
- Working too long hours
- Having to take orders from superiors
- Having to control subordinate staff
- Delegating tasks to others
- Disciplining staff
- Attending meetings
- Addressing meetings
- Handling paperwork
- Accounting for expenses
- Spending too much time away from friends or family

Try applying the following questions to those items which you find most stressful.

- What changes would I like to happen?
- When will I stop this being a limiting factor to my life?

- In how many ways might I solve this?
- How will it feel/look/sound when I've solved it?
- How can I be creative about this?
- What is the worst thing that could happen if I didn't do this?
- If I were to die tomorrow, how would these things be handled?
- What new insights have I got from viewing the problem in these ways?

We choose our joys and sorrows long before
we experience them
– Kahlil Gibran, *Sand and Foam*

Now let's look at the stressors one by one.

- Having too much work.
  [Can I pass any of this work over to anyone else? If not, can I make out a case for additional staff to be employed? Who would handle the work if I were to fall ill/die?]

- Being a slave to addictive behaviour patterns and unhealthy dependence on alcohol, cigarettes, drugs.
  [Can I do more exercise, sleep and eat more regularly, and cut down my unhealthy dependence?]

- Having to work to time constraints or too long hours.
  [Is there some way I can put less pressure on my time? Can I reschedule my timetable?]

- Having to spend too much time travelling to/from/during work.
  [Can I change my hours of work so as to give me more time, say, by reducing travelling time? Can I move home so as to be nearer to work? Can I change jobs to a nearer location?]

- Having to take orders from superiors.
  [How about trying assertiveness training? What would happen if I said "no"? Try imagining the superior in his/her underwear.]

- Having to control subordinate staff.
  [How would I like to be treated in that person's position? Might they find me as unapproachable as I find my superior?]

- Delegating tasks to others.
  [Do I trust the person to whom I am delegating the task? If not, then I am creating more stress for myself. What are my options? Do I find someone else in house? Do I recruit someone else? Do I "bite the bullet" and do the task myself?]

- Disciplining staff.
  [Can I do this in a calm and reasonable way? If not, can I delegate the job? Above all I must remember to be courteous.]

- Attending meetings.
  [What is my main concern? Have I made sure that I have all the information I am likely to need? Remind myself that all the other participants will be equally tense.]

- Addressing meetings.
  [Mental rehearsal. Develop a "State of Excellence" and access it before each meeting.]

- Handling paperwork.
  [Clear the simple things first. It is much easier to cope with papers when the pile has been reduced.]

- Accounting for expenses.
  [Establish a discipline whereby expense claims are prepared within a fixed time of their accrual. Recognise how much stress arises from the delay in dealing with expense claims. Remind myself how good I feel when my expenses are up to date.]

- Spending too much time away from friends or family. Taking work home.
  [MAKE TIME FOR FAMILY AND FRIENDS! Can I start work earlier in order to get home earlier, with my workload completed, before the children are in bed?]

The female experience

Women in the Workplace

The number of women working has increased considerably since World War II, and the number of married women and mothers working has increased dramatically. What many men in the past regarded as a male domain, a sort of men's club, has had its bastions stormed by women. Where men have long accepted women in a subordinate capacity, they have now had to adjust to women filling supervisory and executive roles.

It is inevitable that women will experience more stress than men in the workplace. Those women who seek to combine a demanding career with an equally demanding home life are clearly at risk. There is a tendency for men to regard their home life as a refuge from their occupational stressors, while women are more likely to regard home as a further area of stress. Although there has been some change in male attitudes, a more androgynous approach to the sharing of domestic chores, it is still likely that many men will expect to return from work to a home where their meals will be provided and other household chores done, even when the provider has been spending an equal amount of time at work.

And in addition to the stressors to which men are prey at work, there are many additional pressures placed on women merely by virtue of their gender and their response to the (perceived) problems they pose to employers. Such considerations as reduced physical strength and the possibility that they may have to take maternity leave and subsequently care for their children may have some basis in fact. What is less obvious, because it is at least partially subconscious, is the unease with which some men may regard the possibility of women taking a supervisory role over men, and it is to disguise this unease that they may rationalise their prejudices about women in executive positions.

The efforts of women to hold their own in what was a male preserve, and to demand equal conditions where they show equal capability, can sometimes result in either real or perceived aggressiveness and abrasiveness on their part.

This can be their response to the resentment or resistance that women attract (or feel) from male colleagues, and particularly those who have a subordinate role in the organisation. By contrast men who are overtly aggressive are often admired by their male colleagues who regard this characteristic as a sign of determination and strength.

Although it is easy enough to empathise and sympathise with the stressors to which women are subjected in the workplace, it might be worthwhile to consider also the additional stress placed on men who have to work alongside women, particularly in those areas which were previously regarded as the "male domain". There may also be an additional stress factor to consider in the case of men whose wives are at work and who are required to share household responsibilities for which their upbringing may not have equipped them.

The Menstrual Cycle

From the onset of her menstrual cycle to post-menopause women are subject to a number of physical and, in many cases, emotional influences which are not experienced by men. Many women experience little or no discomfort from the monthly hormonal activity, but others may suffer a variety of symptoms, including fatigue, nervousness, heaviness and ill-temper. There may be a dual aspect to the severity of these symptoms: on the one hand if the woman is obliged to perform her normal tasks and duties without any apparent support or understanding from colleagues or superiors, she may become stressed and the symptoms may become more severe; on the other hand, if she is already in a stressed situation, pre-menstrual tension may increase, and her stress become even more acute.

At the other end of the hormonal scale, there are some women who have no difficulty at all in coping with the onset of the menopause. The menstrual periods gradually diminish and finally cease without any apparent problems. Other women may experience symptoms, of which hot flushes are the most common, which may cause them feelings of acute discomfort and embarrassment, and which may either arise from stress, or result in stress. Giddiness, fatigue, inability to concentrate, and loss of confidence may be other stressors deriving from the menopause.

There are ways of dealing with this situation medically, of which hormone replacement therapy is probably the best known. It is not the intention of the authors to suggest any specific therapy, but merely to plead for greater tolerance in the workplace and in the home in order to reduce the stress which may be experienced.

Give me not excess of it

"Burnout" is the expression used to describe the state of extreme physical and emotional exhaustion resulting from stress at work, and it is insidious. It starts with job satisfaction and ever-increasing effort in fulfilling duties. Too great an expenditure of energy ultimately leads to fatigue and inability to work at the desired or required level. Symptoms of negative tension appear: sleeplessness, headaches, aches and pains, loss of appetite. The symptoms get worse and are accompanied by an inability to relax and a preoccupation with work. Finally, the stress resolves itself into anxiety, depression, and serious health problems. Often it is just one additional factor or event, possibly something which would ordinarily be regarded as quite trivial, which will tip the balance. This is the stage of burnout. It is the price paid by those who continue to strive for achievement despite all the messages being fed to them by their minds, bodies and nervous systems that it may be time to call a halt. Effects may be duodenal ulcers, clinical depression, cardiac arrest.

According to Dr. Carol Cooper [*Surviving at Work*, 1995, Health Education Authority, London] burnout "tends to affect those in caring professions such as nursing, medicine and counselling. Perhaps this is because these people often think of themselves as being indispensable."

The Stress/Performance Curve, on page 87, visually demonstrates this syndrome. At first (the bottom left hand corner of the curve) the job or task is handled with a minimum of stressful effort and produces very satisfactory results. This continues with further effort until performance achieves its optimum effect. At this point the tendency on the part of the "candidate for burnout" is to aim for still greater achievement, ignoring (or not even being aware of) the fatigue that now accompanies the greater effort. At the point of exhaustion the body and the nervous system are yelling "Stop!" and the mind is ignoring the message. The body then takes charge. The point of breakdown is passed; the state of burnout is reached.

I guess it's burnout—whichever way you look at it

What contributes to this point of breakdown? What is responsible for a person who is striving for greater achievement failing to recognise symptoms which would indicate that they have reached a point of diminishing returns, and that persistence will result in breakdown? There is no single, simple answer. It is possible, however, to identify a number of characteristics typical of this situation which, in some cases, symbolise the person's own self-destructive impulses. These include a tendency to depression and to lowered self-esteem. They include also a desire for perfection and success which may be a form of over-compensation for the lack of self-esteem and the tendency to depression. In the caring professions there may be a tendency to identify with the problems of clients or patients, which is one of the dangers people entering these professions are often warned about.

They include also desire for perfection

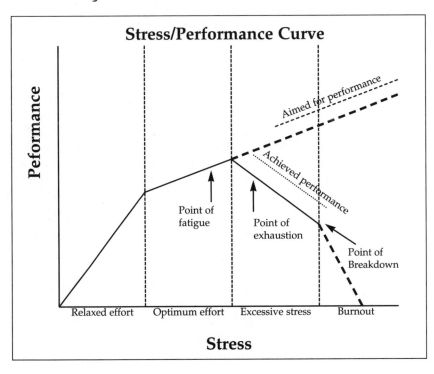

Stress/Performance Curve

Peformance

Aimed for performance

Achieved performance

Point of fatigue

Point of exhaustion

Point of Breakdown

Relaxed effort   Optimum effort   Excessive stress   Burnout

Stress

Having dealt with the effects of work overload at some length in the preceding pages, it is time to study the obverse of that particular coin, and the first thing to note is that – in the appropriate circumstances – work can be therapeutic, and not working can be distressful.

Retirement from work, or unemployment, unless the "leisure" time gained or given is occupied by relatively strenuous mental or physical activity, may result in increased stress and premature death. *No work may be more likely to kill than overwork.* In fact, overwork is a term which has no meaning. It is impossible to work beyond one's capabilities. Work overload is another matter. What is often described as overwork refers rather to the perception the worker has of his or her situation and his/her reaction to it: mentally, physically and emotionally.

Chapter Eight

Self-help And Exercises

Learn to juggle!

Stressbuster
Close your eyes and breathe deeply.
Repeat to yourself:
"Today I shall see nothing but beauty."

I am never upset for the reason I think

Winston Churchill is reputed to have said, "When I look back on all these worries, I remember the story of the old man who said on his deathbed that he had had a lot of trouble in his life, most of which never happened."

Similarly, much of our perceived stress is baggage we carry around with us from force of habit. We have become accustomed to its weight on our shoulders, and maybe we have never considered the possibility that we might confront it, banish it, and find ourselves with a lighter load to bear and a more positive outlook.

Ken Keyes' *Handbook to Higher Consciousness* informs us that... "the only thing I need is the recognition that there's nothing I need that I haven't already got." And, in an apparently different way, but basically expressing the same sentiment, *Attitudinal Healing* (based on *A Course in Miracles*) tells us that we are never upset for the reason we think. And both these statements are particularly relevant in thinking about stress. Perhaps we are never stressed for the reasons we think. Perhaps, indeed, we do not even know the reason for our stress. Perhaps our stress comes from wanting what we already possess.

Perhaps we are never stressed for the reason we think.

**If I knew what was causing my stress,
maybe I wouldn't be so stressed**

Here's a little exercise you might experiment with –
Set yourself a start-of-day target: "Today I shall feel only peace";
"Today I shall see only beauty"; "Today I shall make no judge-
ments". Acknowledge that it will be impossible to retain the
attitude throughout the whole day, but practise reminding
yourself of it during the day by various devices – the knot in the
handkerchief (not recommended if you use paper tissues!), little
note in your pocket or handbag. Award yourself a (mental) gold
star every time you remember your resolution and put it into
effect.

At the end of the day review your experience. Did the experiment result in a reduction of your normally perceived stress level? How often did you remember your target? How often did you forget? Did you notice any significant difference in your stress level on any of those occasions?

Close your eyes and visualise an object that has pleasant conotation.

Another possibility for experimentation: if we accept the premise that stress causes tension, that unresolved tension may lead to anxiety, and that extreme anxiety may require medical attention – then clearly it is better to deal with this at the tension stage, particularly since the tensions may be used in a positive way and provide positive benefits.

What then can we do in this situation?
We can take a break from whatever is perceived as causing the tension. We can lose ourselves in a different activity.

Where this is not possible, we have other options – an immediate possibility being to talk about our stress which, at its most helpful, would be done in a co-counselling situation as described in Chapter Six.

When the tension is perceived as coming from an unbearable work load we can try chunking down, as described in Chapter Seven.

If we recognise the driver/s which may be aggravating the stressful condition we can deal with the BE PERFECT, or TRY HARDER, in some of the ways suggested in Chapter Five.

Finally we could – where the tension comes from a dispute – try giving in!

> ### *Stress is not the culprit; one's vulnerability to stress is*

The type A person, aggressive, competitive, short-tempered and short of patience, as we have already noted (see page 79) is more likely to suffer a coronary than the type B person, even though the latter may be no less ambitious than the former.

The questionnaire which appears on page 95 is designed to demonstrate which of these types you most closely resemble. It is a simple indicator to your beliefs and attitudes. Too much or too little, always or never, may indicate a need to change certain atttudes, aspects of your lifestyle, or even the kind of work you do.

When dealing with day-to-day matters, casual and significant events and relationships, it is important to find a balance between apathetic indifference and enthusiastic involvement.

The Mallows-Sinclair Lifestyle Indicator

I feel OK about making mistakes

Never   Always

I take risks

Never   Always

I act naturally

Never   Always

I show feelings

Never   Always

I ask for help

Never   Always

I admit defeat

Never   Always

I am satisfied with what I do

Never   Always

I can relax

Never   Always

I can be assertive

Never   Always

I believe I matter

Never   Always

I conform/fit in

Never   Always

I can take my time

Never   Always

I can say "No!" appropriately

Never   Always

Strategy for survival

Prevention is usually better than cure!

It will be obvious that we, the authors, believe it better to prepare for, and ideally prevent, stressful situations than to deal with the after-effects. With adequate and appropriate preparation, you are better able to minimise, perhaps eradicate the worst impact of stressful encounters and experiences. It is also useful, and empowering, given that we are almost never upset for the reasons we think, to develop awareness of thoughts, fears and fantasies, what hopes and aspirations lie behind our patterned, less-than-effective behaviours and stress responses.

The following exercise can be used before, although initially it may be easier to use it *after*, an event to explore what is going on beneath the surface.

Each step in the exercise begins with the first words of a statement. You need to complete the sentence/s. Give some thought to what you write. Be wary of editing out what doesn't "suit" you, or the image you have of an idealised Self. It is often the case, precisely because we don't want to listen to the voice of inner truth, that we edit and censor ourselves before an unpalatable thought has a chance to be developed or explored, mined for its richness and potential.

Conversely, you could be so anxious in striving for the perfect answer that you don't allow yourself any answer at all.

This exercise is a self-diagnostic tool. It offers insights into what, in your head, heart and gut, may contribute to your stressful states and relationships.

It can take some practice for you to begin recognising the patterns you run. It will require persistence, a decision to take responsibility for yourself and an ongoing commitment to action, for you to apply the insights as a preventative measure.

Below is the general outline for the exercise. On the following page is a real-life example.

Exercise: Survival Strategies

Complete the following statements *(The words in brackets are intended as useful prompts to help you focus on precise answers.)*:

When I'm feeling not OK *(angry, triumphant, deceitful, envious, avaricious, fearful, lazy, sad, disappointed, helpless, worthless, unlovable)*

I think that other people are *(thinking, feeling, believing, wanting...)*

Those thoughts and feelings make me think that I must *(hurry up, try hard, be strong, be perfect, please others, demand that others please me)*

I am driven in this way because I *(secretly?)* hope, wish *(to get)*

And I also hope to avoid...

These desires result in me *(acting, feeling, saying...)*

I then end up feeling *(sad, mad, scared)*

And I imagine that others *(think, feel, say, do...)*

Example:
Mary has a career and a family. Her two children are "normal" teenagers, stroppy and surly at times, charming and delightful, lazy loafers or energetic enthusiasts. They are not, as far as Mary is aware, into drugs or crime, but they need constant chivvying to get up in the mornings, to go to bed at night, to turn their music below deafening level.

Mary's husband's business takes him out of the country for long periods, so there is always a lot to catch up on when they are together.

Mary is a highly intelligent, creative and caring person who probably gives far too much and asks too little of people.

She puts a lot into making her personal and professional life successful, and is pleased with the way everything melds together.

However, at times she has feelings of not being valued or appreciated at home, and not being acknowledged at work. She was reluctant to say anything to any of the people involved because, she said, it would be unfair and unreasonable to expect them to do anything, so what would be the point?

The following describes Mary's answers to the exercise.

Mary's Strategy at Home
When I'm feeling not OK at home I get frustrated about all the mess I have to clear up after the kids. *I think that they* are completely unaware of how hard I work to make a good life and keep a good home.

Thinking and feeling this, I feel driven to work even *harder* to be the *perfect* mother playing happy families.

I feel driven in this way because I (secretly?) hope they'll see what I'm doing and offer some sort of help or... I'm not saying I want gratitude *(she does, of course)*.

And I also *hope to avoid* upsets and rows and even more frustration.

This results in my believing that I am undervalued, unappreciated and unloved.

I then *end up feeling* bitter, sulking, sad – and then, because I feel guilty, I try even harder at my job to take my mind off what's happening at home.

And I *imagine that the others,* my kids and husband are unaware, indifferent or uncaring.

Mary was surprised when she realised what was going on for her, and decided to do something about it. She told her family that she wanted to discuss something of importance with them. They all went to a restaurant for a meal because, Mary said, she wanted it to be special. After the main course, and before the dessert, she gave each of them a letter, and said they should read it, first privately, then to each other.

The letters described all the things that Mary loved and appreciated about her family. She went into detail, offering descriptive praise – specific examples of what she was celebrating and validating about each of them – and how she valued what they did and who they were.

After each letter had been read out, Mary explained how she had used the Survival Strategy exercise, and the insights she had gained. She owned responsibility for not speaking up, for not risking upsetting them, and for keeping quiet about something that was vitally important to her. She wanted them to know that she valued them, and what she wanted in terms of feeling valued *by* them.

She said she did not want to blame or criticise, but wanted to negotiate how to make things different.

Mary is her own woman, but needed awareness of her own processes in order to take action that would make a difference, not least by reducing her stress levels.

You may be surprised, as Mary was, at some of the answers you get. It is not always easy to recognise, let alone accept, what you discover beneath your dysfunctional, yet all too familiar, patterns of thinking and feeling. Of course, as we have said before, everything you do originally had a positive intent. Stress responses are intended to protect us against real or imagined threats to our well-being.

Stress responses that build into distress patterns are archaic; they do not serve us well.

This survival strategy exercise should be considered a first aid measure, a first step toward greater health and responsibility, towards reduced negative stress, and towards increased emotional intelligence.

Taking it further, making it more a way of life than a mere exercise, for example, devising other, more effective, less stressful strategies for connecting and communicating with yourself and other people, is the subject of another book in this series. However, you can make a start by asking, *"What other, less manipulative or "gamey" ways are there for getting my needs met?"*

It is not easy to ask, in a direct, open, honest way, for people to respond to our unstated needs, especially if we are not aware of them ourselves. We can, however, become aware that we have been asking the wrong questions of the wrong people at the wrong time.

The survival strategy exercise often precludes the need to keep asking, or enables us to ask in more direct, clear, authentic and self-validating ways.

And, of course, because you are less stressed, you may ask with greater clarity and compassion, and wait with more patience and equanimity, giving others a chance to make amends or adjustments, if they so wish.

And Finally: A Few Simple Stress-Defeating Strategies

- Don't make mountains out of molehills. Ask yourself: "What's the worst thing that could happen?"
- Learn to recognise signals from your body, your mind, your nervous system. Identify where they come from. Teach yourself some coping skills to deal with signals heralding the onset of a stressful situation.
- Praise yourself whenever you accomplish something positive, no matter how small. Look for opportunities to identify positive achievement. When feeling the onset of a stressful situation, recall one of the moments of positive achievement and award yourself a merit badge.
- It is better to rant and scream when you are feeling OK rather than when you are feeling upset. Try letting out a few healthy yells when you feel good. If you can identify the yelling with feeling good, maybe it will be harder to aggravate your emotional state by raving when you are feeling upset.
- When you are beside yourself, remember Groucho Marx's advice: "Move over. You're in bad company."
- Do not let stress undermine your sense of personal worth and dignity. Learn assertiveness.
- Learn to juggle!

Crown House Publishing Limited

Crown Buildings,
Bancyfelin,
Carmarthen, Wales, UK, SA33 5ND.
Telephone: +44 (0) 1267 211880
Facsimile: +44 (0) 1267 211882
e-mail: crownhouse@anglo-american.co.uk
Website: www.anglo-american.co.uk

We trust you enjoyed this title from our range of bestselling books for professional and general readership. All our authors are professionals of many years' experience, and all are highly respected in their own field. We choose our books with care for their content and character, and for the value of their contribution of both new and updated material to their particular field. Here is a list of all our other publications.

Change Management Excellence: *Putting NLP To Work In The 21st Century*
by Martin Roberts PhD   Hardback   £25.00

Ericksonian Approaches: *A Comprehensive Manual*
by Rubin Battino & Thomas L South PhD   Hardback   £25.00

Figuring Out People: *Design Engineering With Meta-Programs*
by Bob G. Bodenhamer & L. Michael Hall   Paperback   £12.99

Gold Counselling™: *A Practical Psychology With NLP*
by Georges Philips & Lyn Buncher   Paperback   £14.99

Grieve No More, Beloved: *The Book Of Delight*
by Ormond McGill   Hardback   £9.99

Hypnotherapy Training In The UK: *An Investigation Into The Development Of
   Clinical Hypnosis Training Post-1971*
by Shaun Brookhouse   Spiralbound   £9.99

Influencing With Integrity: *Management Skills For Communication & Negotiation*
by Genie Z Laborde   Paperback   £12.50

The Magic Of Mind Power: *Awareness Techniques For The Creative Mind*
by Duncan McColl   Paperback   £8.99

A Multiple Intelligences Road To An ELT Classroom
by Michael Berman   Paperback   £19.99

Multiple Intelligences Poster Set
by Jenny Maddern   Nine posters   £19.99

The New Encyclopedia Of Stage Hypnotism
by Ormond McGill   Hardback   £29.99

NOW It's Your Turn For Success! *Training And Motivational Techniques For Direct Sales And
   Multi-Level Marketing*
by Richard Houghton and Janet Kelly   Paperback   £9.99

The POWER Process: *An NLP Approach To Writing*
by Sid Jacobson & Dixie Elise Hickman   Paperback   £12.99

Precision Therapy: *A Professional Manual Of Fast And Effective Hypnoanalysis Techniques*
by Duncan McColl PhD   Paperback   £15.00

Scripts & Strategies In Hypnotherapy
by Roger P. Allen   Hardback   £19.99

Order form

*******Special offer: 4 for the price of 3!!!*******

Buy 3 books & we'll give you a 4th title - FREE!
(free title will be book of lowest value)

Qty	Title	Qty	Title
—	Change Management Excellence	—	The POWER Process
—	Ericksonian Approaches	—	Precision Therapy
—	Figuring Out People	—	Scripts & Strategies In Hypnotherapy
—	Gold Counselling™	—	The Secrets Of Magic
—	Grieve No More, Beloved	—	Seeing The Unseen
—	Hypnotherapy Training In The UK	—	Slimming With Pete
—	Influencing With Integrity	—	Smoke-Free And No Buts!
—	The Magic Of Mind Power	—	Solution States
—	A Multiple Intelligences Road To An ELT	—	The Sourcebook Of Magic
	Classroom	—	The Spirit Of NLP
—	Multiple Intelligences Poster Set	—	Sporting Excellence
—	New Encyclopedia Of Stage Hypnotism	—	Time-Lining
—	Now It's YOUR Turn For Success!	—	The User's Manual For The Brain
—	Peace Of Mind Is A Piece Of Cake	—	Vibrations For Health And Happiness

Postage and packing

UK:	£2.50 per book
	£4.50 for two or more books
Europe:	£3.50 per book
Rest of the world	£4.50 per book

My details:

Name: Mr/Mrs/Ms/Other (please specify) ....

Address: ....

....

....

Postcode: ....Daytime tel: ....

I wish to pay by:

❏ Amex   ❏ Visa   ❏ Mastercard   ❏ Switch – Issue no./Start date: ....

Card number:...Expiry date:...

Name on card:...Signature:...

❏ cheque/postal order payable to **AA Books**

Please send me the following catalogues:

❏ Accelerated Learning (Teaching Resources)   ❏ Psychotherapy/Counselling
❏ Accelerated Learning (Personal Growth)   ❏ Employment Development
❏ Neuro-Linguistic Programming   ❏ Business
❏ NLP Video Library – hire (UK only)   ❏ Freud
❏ NLP Video Library – sales   ❏ Jung
❏ Ericksonian Hypnotherapy   ❏ Transactional Analysis
❏ Classical Hypnosis   ❏ Parenting
❏ Gestalt Therapy   ❏ Special Needs

Please fax/send to:
The Anglo American Book Company,
FREEPOST SS1340
Crown Buildings, Bancyfelin,
Carmarthen, West Wales,
United Kingdom, SA33 4ZZ,
Tel: +44 (0) 1267 211880/211886 Fax: +44 (0) 1267 211882
or e-mail your order to:
crownhouse@anglo-american.co.uk